Managing Editor
Mara Ellen Guckian

Illustrator
Kelly McMahon

Editor in Chief
Ina Massler Levin, M.A.

Creative Director
Karen J. Goldfluss, M.S. Ed.

Cover Artist
Barb Lorseyedi

Art Coordinator
Renée Mc Elwee

Imaging
James Edward Grace
Rosa C. See
Craig Gunnell

Publisher

Mary D. Smith, M.S. Ed.

TCR 3024

YEAR R... ...DES K–K

Project-Based Activities

FOR

STEM

SCIENCE · TECHNOLOGY · ENGINEERING · MATH

INCLUDES STANDARDS, BENCHMARKS, & OBJECTIVES

Florist

10

Teacher Created Resources

Author

Kathryn Kurowski

The classroom teacher may reproduce the materials in this book and/or CD for use in a single classroom only. The reproduction of any part of this book and/or CD for other classrooms or for an entire school or school system is strictly prohibited. No part of this publication may be transmitted or recorded in any form without written permission from the publisher with the exception of electronic material, which may be stored on the purchaser's computer only.

Teacher Created Resources
6421 Industry Way
Westminster, CA 92683
www.teachercreated.com

ISBN: 978-1-4206-3024-4

© 2013 Teacher Created Resources
Made in U.S.A.

Teacher Created Resources

Table of Contents

Introduction to STEM

As educators, we are being required to place more emphasis on science, technology, engineering, and math (STEM) to ensure that today's students will be prepared for college and the careers of tomorrow. Additionally, practicing important 21st century skills including collaboration, critical thinking, problem solving, and digital literacy should be part of our daily curricula. It is imperative AND a tall order. *Year Round Project-Based Activities for STEM* provides students with needed practice in these areas.

Project-based learning units encourage students to be creative by imagining, inventing, implementing, and improving their own ideas while collaborating with others. Project-based centers can be established to address all manner of themes that include opportunities to perform STEM-related tasks.

The authentic units in this book are comprised of scaffolded activities leading to "play" centers designed and created by students for their own use. Naturally, teachers will provide a great deal of "behind-the-scenes" help. Each unit includes suggested science-, technology-, engineering-, and math-based activities. The project-based process that drives the activities in each unit is a key component to developing 21st century skills as well as competency in the STEM subject areas. Once learned, these skills become life skills that can be used in any situation.

Each 5-phase unit follows a similar pattern that involves a series of student brainstorming sessions followed by hands-on activities. Activities and time frames can be adjusted to meet student needs. Specific STEM tie-ins are provided for each activity. Suggestions are provided for each phase to help teachers tailor projects to student interests. Opportunities for parent support are included throughout.

APR 0 8 2014

Why Project-based Learning?

The classroom is the perfect place to introduce project-based learning, incorporating both academic and 21st century skills, because it is filled with students bubbling with different abilities, backgrounds, and ideas. What's more, project-based activities are fun, and the learning comes naturally. Play is work for young learners, and this book will provide many opportunities to learn "on the job." These experiences will broaden students' world views, encourage them to think critically, and be proactive.

Project-based learning, simply put, is *learning-by-doing*. Project-based learning, or PBL, tends to be deeper learning that is more relevant to students and thus remembered longer. We need to educate students to be global competitors, and to do so, we must require them to think creatively, to take risks, and to put what they are learning into practice.

In STEM curriculum, project-based learning is a must! Its collaborative style guarantees that 21st century skills are incorporated into the curriculum while supporting students' academic and socio-emotional growth. Furthermore, PBL allows teachers to assess what students comprehend immediately, and adapt the curriculum accordingly. Most of all, it is fun!

Why Project-based Learning? *(cont.)*

The units in *Year Round Project-Based Activities for STEM* provide students, teachers, and parents with the following:

Opportunities for critical thinking

The goal is to find the best solution, not the one "right" answer. Open-ended questions or prompts lead to higher-level thinking and encourage investigation. "Unlikely" ideas are sometimes the most valuable or lead to other ideas and should be included during brainstorming. They promote serious thought—Will that work? Why or why not? Let's try it.

Development of organizational skills

Students implement new ideas by learning to plan, to sequence (scaffold) activities, and to self regulate while working with others.

Options for creativity

The units encourage innovative strategies or solutions by stressing the importance of trying new things and of trial and error. (Many great ideas and inventions are the result of failed experiments.)

Practice communicating

The focus is on sharing ideas, theories, and discoveries using appropriate vocabulary and to demonstrate understanding through drawings, graphs, charts, etc.

Relevance

The activities relate to students' lives and make the concepts being taught more meaningful. Ideally, certain activities will foster global awareness and will extend beyond the classroom.

Time for collaborations

The units promote social learning in the classroom and via technology by encouraging students to observe, think critically, and share ideas in a supportive environment.

Suggestions for developing digital literacy

This book provides an environment in which technology is used for research and design and as a tool for student engagement.

Using the units described in this book will help you get a feel for what project-based learning is all about so that you can develop future PBL units with a deeper understanding of the process. Listen. What do your students *want* to learn about, and how can that interest be facilitated? STEM activities can be incorporated into any theme. Templates are provided on pages 111–112 to help you create your own units.

Websites for Project-Based Activities

The following websites offer background information and images which may be helpful in developing the STEM units in this book. The sites may also provide ideas for setting up suggested areas and/or props, related activities, or games.

Safety Alert: Always check websites to make certain the address or content has not changed, that they are age-appropriate, and that they suit your students' current needs.

Repurpose Cardboard Boxes into Kid Crafts/Toys:

http://declutterorganizerepurpose.wordpress.com/2011/02/28/repurpose-cardboard-boxes-into-kid-craftstoys/

Here are some great ideas for repurposing cardboard boxes using recycled materials and items around the home or school. These simple projects can be made for, with, or by students depending on time and skill levels. Encourage creativity and imagination—make cars, gas pumps, stoves, etc.!

Primary Games: *http://www.primarygames.com/fractions/question1.htm*

A variety of games and activities for science, math, social studies, or language arts are provided. There are also sections on transportation that may prove useful for the Airport Unit.

Invention at Play: *http://www.inventionatplay.org/playhouse_main.html*

The Smithsonian Institute's Lemelson Center for the Study of Invention and Innovation provides ideas and video examples of ways to encourage visual thinking, problem solving, tinkering, and collaboration. Additionally there is a section dedicated to historic and contemporary inventors sharing ideas about how they got started.

Science Net Links: *http://www.sciencenetlinks.com/lessons*

Timely science activities and lesson plans for K–12 students are provided in an easy-to-follow manner, along with suggestions for assessment and extensions.

Springboard Magazine: *http://www.springboardmagazine.com*

Explore, create and learn via games and activities for young learners. Advanced students can play the Grocery Store Game (see the math section) in which they purchase items and add their totals.

Thinkfinity: *http://community.thinkfinity.org*

Start with the forum for parents and educators on current educational topics of interest, including STEM. Move on to other areas of the site to enhance student learning through videos, online games or activities.

Ted-Ed: *http://ed.ted.com*

Check out the Lessons Worth Sharing Videos and You Tube connections provided to enhance knowledge of STEM unit topics and perhaps to find age-appropriate student videos.

Websites for Individual STEM Units

Airport

Five-Year-Olds Pilot Their Own Project-Based Learning:

http://www.edutopia.org/kindergarten-project-based-learning-video

Take a look at what your learners can create using "found" materials. With adult help, students can create a "working" airport.

TSA Travel Assistant: *http://www.tsa.gov*

This site updates regularly. You can find answers for all types of airport questions. You might start with information on screening or different jobs. Don't forget to check what is new!

Auto Repair Shop

Kids Car and Truck Auto Repair-You Tube:

http://www.youtube.com/watch?v=2nA0cDlAuw0

This video showcases three children (family) doing basic repairs on a car.

Vics Auto: *http://www.vicsauto.net*

Go to the Anatomy section to view schematic drawings of the underside of a car, the dashboard, battery, etc.

Bowling Alley

SI for Kids Bowling Game: *http://www.sikids.com/games/fun-lanes-bowling*

It takes a little practice, but this game is simple and the results are immediate. Use it as a demo or let students bowl a few frames!

Tom and Jerry Games:

http://www.tomandjerrygames.ws/play-366-Tom-And-Jerry-Bowling-game.html

Another simple, fast-paced bowling game. Even if you don't score well, you get the idea of sending a ball down the lane to hit the pins and then seeing the scores, not to mention the sound effects! (Note: This site provides games for a wide range of ages and interests.

Flower Shop

Family Fun: *http://familyfun.go.com/crafts/fantasy-flower-shop-675317/*

This is a great site for ideas to set up an age-appropriate flower shop. Get ideas for flowers and props. Then, check out the rest of the Family Fun site for other great ideas!

Grocery Store

PBS Kids–Arthur Supermarket Adventure:

http://pbskids.org/arthur/games/supermarket/index.html

In this game, students can help familiar characters shop by dragging food items into the cart.

Ice Fishing

BRRR It is Cold Outside: *http://staff.bbhcsd.org/gagnem/brrr2010.htm*

This site offers detailed directions for making fancy snowflake crystals using pipe cleaners and Borax. The directions are accompanied by pictures of students working on the various stages.

Paper Plate Fish: *http://www.makeandtakes.com/paper-plate-tropicalfish*

Paper Bag Fish: *http://www.tappi.org/paperu/art_class/paperbagfish.htm*

This simple craft idea for making fish is fun to do and allows for student creativity.

Take a Kid Ice Fishing: *http://icefishingtoday.com/pages/episode_take_a_kid_ice_fishing.php*

Vexilar's Ice Fishing Today offers an opportunity to see the sport of ice fishing from start to finish. Learn about the clothes worn and equipment used, the different types of shelters and tools, and see fish caught! This series of videos provides everything you need to know, especially if you do not live in an area where ice fishing is possible. Some sections would be great to share with students, too, to get the ideas flowing. Start with the video called Take a Kid Ice Fishing.

Pizza Parlor

Daily Dress up Games:

http://www.dailydressupgames.com/file.php?f=3322&a=popup

The free game Cooking Show Pizza is fast paced but does involve the step-by-step creation of a pizza.

Veterinarian's Office

Healthy Pet: *http://www.healthypet.com/kidsklub/KidArticles.aspx*

This site offers kid-friendly answers to many questions about being a veterinarian and about caring for pets.

Getting Started

Start with an idea (one of these units) and a useable area in the room. As you figure out what will be feasible, images of what the final product should look like may begin to form in your mind. Don't become too attached to these ideas, though; your students should be the engineers. The five phases in each unit center around student brainstorming and collaboration. These phases may take a day or a week and may overlap.

Nurture creativity and encourage students to be supportive of each other's suggestions. In the beginning, you may have to prod students to share their thoughts since many may feel there is only one "right" answer. Students can be fearful of sharing their ideas lest they be "wrong." Collaborating comfortably to share ideas takes time, but it is a very important 21st century skill to develop.

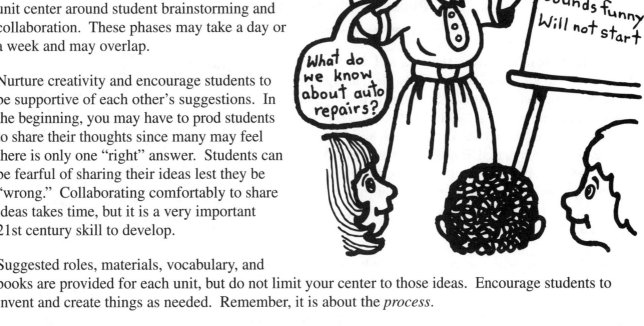

Suggested roles, materials, vocabulary, and books are provided for each unit, but do not limit your center to those ideas. Encourage students to invent and create things as needed. Remember, it is about the *process*.

Getting Started *(cont.)*

> **Phase 1**—Set Up the Center
>
> **Phase 2**—Create Props
>
> **Phase 3**—Define Roles
>
> **Phase 4**—Open the Center
>
> **Phase 5**—Improve the Center

In **Phase 1**, the building phase, students will decide what their area should look like, create a floor plan, and gather and create décor and furniture. For instance, if you plan to make a restaurant, how many tables do you need? Discuss materials in the classroom that can be used, and others that might need to be purchased, borrowed, or created. Maintain ongoing webs, charts, and lists to generate continuing input. Your young engineers and builders will draw and present maps, architectural plans, and other types of graphics to develop the plans for the space.

In **Phase 2**, students will research and create tools or props to make the space functional. These tools may be anything from menus to procedures for operating on a stuffed animal. In one unit they will make an airplane! Students might figure out a way to turn a wagon into a delivery car for a pizza parlor or make a gurney for (stuffed) pet patients. They will learn to draw upon their own experiences to come up with inventive ideas and solutions.

Students will plan jobs and outfit workers/participants in **Phase 3**. If they are creating a business, they will figure out how many employees will be needed, what those employees will need in order to do their jobs, and how many customers can be helped at a time. Students may surprise you as they become comfortable with this phase—both in their understanding of the need to respect participants' personal space (logistics/crowd control) and to establish rules (management) for each activity.

In **Phase 4**, students will put the finishing touches on their creations, and then they will try the new center out. First, they will visualize how it will work. They will rehearse and invite guests. Then, they will use the tools and procedures they have created. They will experiment with and test their inventions.

Finally, in **Phase 5**, students will come back together to evaluate and improve the area they have created. They will discuss what works and what doesn't, and they will adjust their props and procedures. Students will continue to enjoy the space they have created, upgrading and modifying as they see fit.

Standards, Benchmarks, and Learning Objectives

Each lesson in *Year Round Project Based Activities for STEM* (Pre K–K) meets one or more of the following standards for Science, Technology, and Mathematics, which are used with permission from McREL (Copyright 2012 McREL, Mid-continent Research for Education and Learning. Telephone 303-337-0990. Website *www.mcrel.com*). To align McREL Standards to the Common Core Standards go to *www.mcrel.org*. Additionally, age-appropriate learning objectives have been suggested for Engineering.

Science

Understands atmospheric processes and the water cycle

➡ Knows that water can be a liquid or a solid and can be made to change from one form to the other, but the amount of water stays the same

Understands the composition and structure of the universe and the Earth's place in it

➡ Knows basic patterns of the Sun and Moon (e.g., the Sun appears every day and the Moon appears sometimes at night and sometimes during the day; the Sun and Moon appear to move from east to west across the sky; the Moon appears to change shape over the course of a month; the Sun's position in the sky changes through the seasons)

Understands the principles of heredity and related concepts

➡ Knows that plants and animals closely resemble their parents

➡ Knows that differences exist among individuals of the same kind of plant or animal

Understands the structure and function of cells and organisms

➡ Knows the basic needs of plants and animals (e.g., air, water, nutrients, light or food, shelter)

Understands relationships among organisms and their physical environment

➡ Knows that plants and animals need certain resources for energy and growth (e.g., food, water, light, air)

➡ Knows that living things are found almost everywhere in the world and that distinct environments support the life of different types of plants and animals

Understands biological evolution and the diversity of life

➡ Knows that there are similarities and differences in the appearance and behavior of plants and animals

Understands the structure and properties of matter

➡ Knows that different objects are made up of many different types of materials (e.g., cloth, paper, wood, metal) and have many different observable properties (e.g., color, size, shape, weight)

Standards, Benchmarks, and Learning Objectives

Science *(cont.)*

Understands the sources and properties of energy

➡ Knows that the Sun supplies heat and light to Earth

➡ Knows that electricity in circuits can produce light, heat, sound, and magnetic effects

➡ Knows that sound is produced by vibrating objects

Understands forces and motion

➡ Knows that the position of an object can be described by locating it relative to another object or the background

➡ Knows that the position and motion of an object can be changed by pushing or pulling

➡ Knows that things move in many different ways (e.g., straight line, zigzag, vibration, circular motion)

Understands the nature of scientific knowledge

➡ Knows that scientific investigations generally work the same way in different places and normally product results that can be duplicated

Understands the nature of scientific inquiry

➡ Understands the scientific enterprise

➡ Knows that in science it is helpful to work with a team and share findings with others

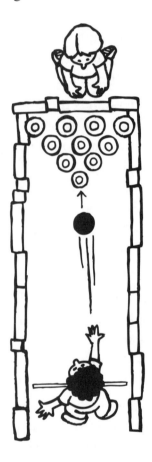

Standards, Benchmarks, and Learning Objectives *(cont.)*

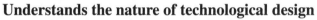

Technology

Knows the characteristics and uses of computer hardware and operating systems

➡ Knows basic computer hardware (e.g., keyboard and mouse, printer and monitor, optical storage device [such as CD-ROM], case for the CPU [central processing unit])

Knows the characteristics and uses of computer software programs

➡ Knows basic features of computer software (e.g., file, open, save, help, preview)

Understands the relationships among science, technology, society, and the individual

➡ Knows ways that technology is used at home and at school (e.g., computers, cell phones, cameras, DVD players)

Understands the nature of technological design

➡ Knows that tools have specific functions, such as to observe, measure, make things, and do things better or more easily; selecting the right tool makes the task easier

Engineering

Students will use engineering design to pose questions, seek answers, and develop solutions

➡ Identifies simple problems and solutions

➡ Proposes alternative solutions for procedures

➡ Understands elements of production planning

➡ Understands troubleshooting procedures

➡ Uses tools, materials, and equipment associated with the building trades

➡ Understands elements of planning construction projects

➡ Uses skills and techniques related to building, maintaining, and repairing structures

➡ Uses a variety of verbal and graphic techniques to present conclusions

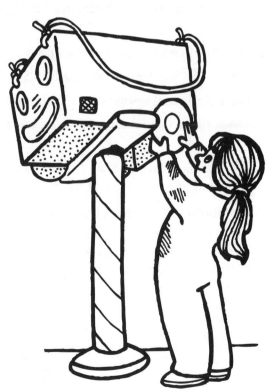

Standards, Benchmarks, and Learning Objectives *(cont.)*

Math

Uses a variety of strategies in the problem-solving process

- ➡ Uses discussions with teachers and other students to understand problems
- ➡ Makes organized lists or tables of information necessary for solving a problem

Understands and applies basic and advanced properties of the concepts of numbers

- ➡ Counts whole numbers (i.e., both cardinal and ordinal numbers)
- ➡ Understands symbolic, concrete, and pictorial representations of numbers (e.g., written numerals, objects in sets, number lines)

Uses basic and advanced procedures while performing the processes of computation

- ➡ Knows that the quantity of objects can change by adding or taking away objects
- ➡ Adds and subtracts whole numbers
- ➡ Solves real-world problems involving addition and subtraction of whole numbers
- ➡ Understands basic estimation strategies (e.g., using reference sets, using front-end digits) and terms (e.g., "about," "near," "closer to," "between," "a little less than")

Understands and applies basic and advanced properties of the concepts of measurement

- ➡ Understands the basic measures of length, width, height, weight, and temperature

Understands and applies basic and advanced concepts of statistics and data analysis

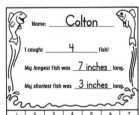

- ➡ Collects and represents information about objects or events in simple graphs
- ➡ Understands that one can find out about a group of things by studying just a few of them

Understands and applies basic and advanced concepts of probability

- ➡ Understands that some events can be predicted fairly well but others cannot because we do not always know everything that may affect an event

STEM in the Airport

science

Physics—Explore how planes stay in the air and how machines "see" into suitcases. What is an X-ray?

Weather—Learn about changing weather conditions and how they might affect flying.

Safety—Discover the importance of security in an airport and on a flight.

echnology

Internet Research—Find information about airports and airplanes. Learn about airport machines such as security scanners, baggage conveyor belts, etc. Research items relevant to airplanes like the cockpit, seats, overhead storage, beverage carts, seat belts, luggage, and other possible props.

Desktop Publishing—Make boarding passes, signage, passports and identification, postcards, luggage tags, and name tags for workers.

ngineering

Drawing—Plan and map out the layout for the classroom airport. Include the check-in station, a security checkpoint, and baggage claim. Plan and map out the cockpit, flight attendant service area, and seating on the airplane.

Creating Spaces—Arrange the airport and airplane using classroom furniture and other materials at hand.

Designing—Make cockpit control panels using different craft materials, computers for check-in, and security wands. Don't forget tickets, boarding passes, passports, etc.

Collaborating and Problem Solving—Discuss the roles and expectations for those working at the airport, in the airplane, and for the travelers as well. Why are safety issues so important?

ath

Numbers—Count the number of workers needed, the number of travelers, and pieces of luggage. Create seat numbers and try boarding by calling out ordinal numbers.

Sequencing—Determine the air travel process from ticket purchase to arrival.

Size and Measurement—Compare luggage sizes—greater than or less than; small, medium, large, extra large; heavy, light.

Time—Determine times and durations for flights.

Addition and Subtraction—Calculate the number of travelers or pieces of luggage.

Money—Establish prices for flights, extra luggage, etc.

Market Research—Chart and graph the number of visitors to the different destinations each week. Determine the most popular destination in the class airport.

Airport Starters

Suggested Props and Materials

- ○ briefcases, suitcases, and purses
- ○ cardboard boxes (including pizza boxes)
- ○ cash registers and play money
- ○ chairs, tables, shelving
- ○ clipboards
- ○ Control Panel Gauges template (page 21)
- ○ dress-up clothes and other items that would be packed in suitcases
- ○ empty food containers and play food
- ○ flashlights
- ○ globe
- ○ keyboards and old computers
- ○ maps, travel brochures
- ○ Name Tags template (page 23)
- ○ paper for labels, signs, tags, boarding passes
- ○ Pilot/Security Hat template (page 24)
- ○ pipe cleaners for luggage tags
- ○ plastic trays and cups
- ○ scale to weigh suitcases
- ○ steering wheel (real or created)
- ○ wagon or cart
- ○ walkie-talkies, phones, headphones

Others

_____

_____

_____

_____

_____

Airport Starters *(cont.)*

Vocabulary

air traffic controller

airbus

aircraft

airplane

airport code

baggage

blimp

boarding pass

carry-on

checkpoint

cockpit

control tower

controls

conveyor belt

co-pilot

flight attendant

helicopter

identification

jet

license

luggage

passenger

passport

pilot

runway

scanner

security

standby

tarmac

ticketing agents

traveler

TSA officers

Others

_____

_____

_____

_____

_____

_____

Books

A Day at an Airport by Sarah Harrison

What Happens at an Airport? by Amy Hutchings

Airplanes by Mary Lindeen

Airplanes by Cynthia Roberts

Others

_____

_____

_____

The Airport Plan

Phase 1: Set Up the Airport

Students will:

- graph experiences with airplanes and airports
- research and design a classroom airport
- gather and arrange boxes and other materials to create a security checkpoint, a check-in counter/ticketing area, baggage, and a baggage claim area
- maintain a word wall
- name the airport and create signage

Phase 2: Make the Cockpit, Service Area, and Seating

Students will:

- establish areas for the cockpit, service area, and seating in the airplane
- construct the cockpit controls using materials such as bottle caps, blocks, magnets, old electronics parts, etc.
- set up a speaker system to allow the pilot to talk to the tower and crew, and the crew to talk to passengers
- create an area for the flight crew and a system for serving snacks

Phase 3: Define Roles

Students will:

- research types of workers needed to run an airport
- formulate job descriptions; try different roles
- gather or make wardrobe items and prop materials
- determine the number of workers and travelers; make sign-ups
- create identification, boarding passes, tickets, luggage stickers, and signs

Phase 4: Open the Airport

Students will:

- vote on five favorite destinations and research the airports for these destinations; decide which locations will become the destination for the day (rotate the five favorites) and determine departure times
- practice arriving at the ticketing counter, checking baggage, and going through security toward the boarding area
- practice boarding the plane, piloting the plane, serving travelers
- check the weather and officially open the airport for business

Phase 5: Improve the Airport

Students will:

- evaluate what worked and what needs adjusting
- initiate improvements based on discussions and research
- enjoy the newly created airport and expand and improve as desired

The Airport

Phase 1: Set Up the Airport

1. What do we know about airports? Why do people go to airports? Who has been to an airport?

2. What is the order that customers need to follow to travel from one place to another on a plane? (purchase ticket–check in–check luggage–security check–board–deplane–gather luggage.)

3. Start a list of terms pertinent to the airport. Continue to add to it as the airport takes shape. Post the words on a word wall so students can copy them as needed.

4. Vote on a name for the airport.

Student STEM Activities

1. Research airports and airport towers and provide pictures when possible. Share data. Create a sign for the airport. (***Technology/Math***)

2. Gather materials and classroom furniture to set up the airport based on the brainstorming sessions. Collaborate and determine what is needed, what will fit, and where it will go. (***Technology/Engineering/Math***)

3. Improvise, arrange, and embellish items to create stations for ticketing agents and baggage check-in. Don't forget to weigh and sort luggage! Is it too big for carry-on? Set aside a box for measuring the size of carry-on luggage. (***Technology/Engineering/Math***)

4. Design a security checkpoint. A large refrigerator-sized box works well for students to pass through. (***Science/Technology/Engineering/Math***)

5. Devise a baggage scanner. A box with the ends removed and placed on top of a construction paper or fabric conveyor belt works well. (***Science/Technology/Engineering/Math***)

Teacher Support

1. Listen and record student responses during brainstorming sessions. Create a list of reasons to go to the airport or a graph of who has and has not been to an airport. Offer encouragement and provide reasonable amounts of time for research, planning, and creating.

2. Fill the classroom with related books, travel brochures and tickets, pictures, and posters. Include student contributions as they are created.

3. Provide opportunities for students to discover that luggage is made in different shapes, sizes, and colors. Magazines and the Internet are good resources. Demonstrate how to use a scale to determine the weight and a box to check carry-on size.

4. Create word cards for a pocket chart or a word wall. Keep adding pertinent vocabulary words as they come up. (See page 17.)

5. Call a local travel agent for possible donations. See if the local airport can accommodate field trips.

6. Ask parents to donate or gather materials or to help with assembly to get the airport going. Invite parents in related industries to come in and share their work experiences.

The Airport *(cont.)*

Phase 2: Make the Cockpit, Service Area, and Seating

1. Do surveys. Who has been on an airplane? Where have they traveled? Where would students like to go?

2. Start a discussion about the type of items on the airplane. How many seats should be in the cockpit? How can a control panel be made? How will the pilot speak to the crew and passengers? Where will the passengers sit, and where should luggage go?

Student STEM Activities

1. Research airplanes and their interiors. Share data and print pictures. (*Science/Technology*)

2. Establish the area that will serve as the airplane. Figure out how many seats should be on either side of the aisle, and how many rows of seats there will be. Create seat numbers and signs (No Smoking, Seatbelts Fastened, etc.). (*Science/Technology/Engineering/Math*)

3. Create a cockpit complete with a control panel and communication system.

   Suggestion: Collect and sort caps from milk, soda, water, etc. Glue them to cardboard to create cockpit controls. Additional control panel ideas can be found on page 21. (*Science/Technology/Engineering/Math*)

4. Design a communication system for the pilot to talk to the crew and the crew to talk to passengers. (*Science/Technology*)

5. Set up the flight crew area. Perhaps a wagon or cart can be used for beverage or snack service during flights. (*Technology/Engineering/Math*)

Teacher Support

1. Assist with charting destinations where students have traveled or would like to travel. Encourage them to select the top five to be used for destinations for their class airport.

2. Assist with finding materials for the control panels or provide patterns. See if old electronic equipment might be donated and used. Anything with buttons, knobs, microphones, or switches will enhance the airplane or the airport.

3. Offer encouragement and provide reasonable amounts of time for research, planning, and creating.

The Airport *(cont.)*

Control Panel Gauges

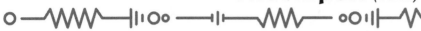

The Airport *(cont.)*

Phase 3: Define Roles

Construction is underway and the airport and airplane need a staff and passengers.

1. Discuss each job and list the responsibilities attached to it. What skills would each worker need to be successful? Does a pilot need to know the same things as a ticket agent? How about a security person? How do weather conditions affect flying?

2. Figure out wardrobe items or props for each job. What do you need to board a plane? (ticket, identification, boarding pass)

Student STEM Activities

1. Research airport jobs, share data, and collect and display pictures.
   (***Science/Technology/Engineering/Math***)

2. Gather materials to create and store the props and wardrobe items for each role. Improvise and create additional props using classroom materials and imagination! (***Science/Technology/Engineering/Math***)

3. Create labels or name tags for each position. (See page 23 for samples.) Consider making time sheets for workers and sign-up sheets for travelers. (***Technology/Math***)

4. Dramatize different roles. Note how often airport workers use math—weighing luggage, counting passengers, paying for tickets, flight times, etc. (***Technology/Math***)

5. Use weather information and wall maps to track actual flight patterns to the destinations chosen. (***Science/Technology/Math***)

6. Create identification, boarding passes, passports, luggage tickets (can be attached with a hole punch and pipe cleaners), and signs. (***Technology/Math***)

Teacher Support

1. Review the list of jobs and their responsibilities and provide wardrobe or prop ideas. If pilot or security hats are unavailable, adjust the pattern on page 24 to suit, laminate it, and attach strips of paper to the sides. Adjust the strips to the child's head and staple ends to create a hat.

2. Model roles students might not be familiar with based on brainstorming discussions. Stress that good service is important. Also emphasize the benefits of taking turns.

The Airport *(cont.)*

Name Tags

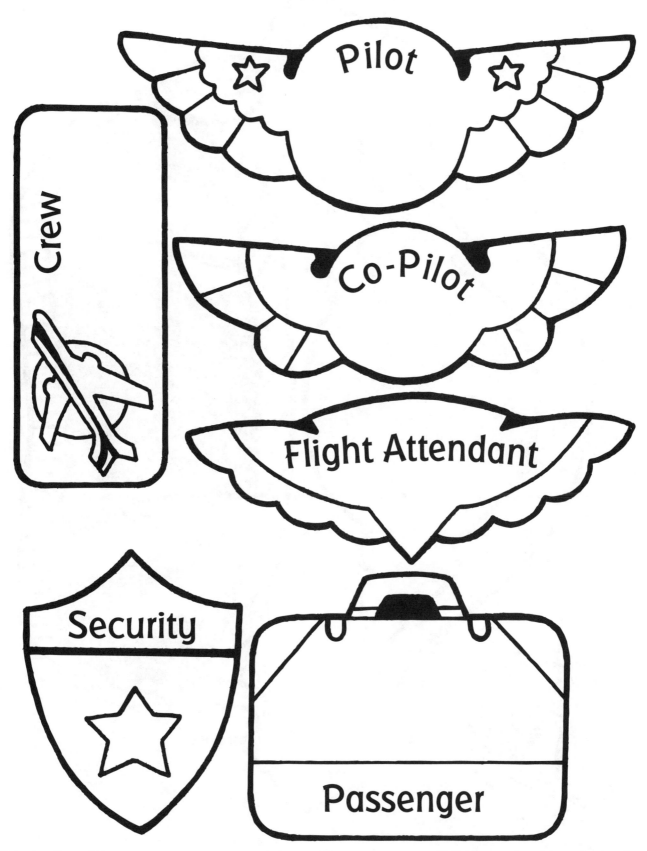

The Airport *(cont.)*

Pilot/Security Hat

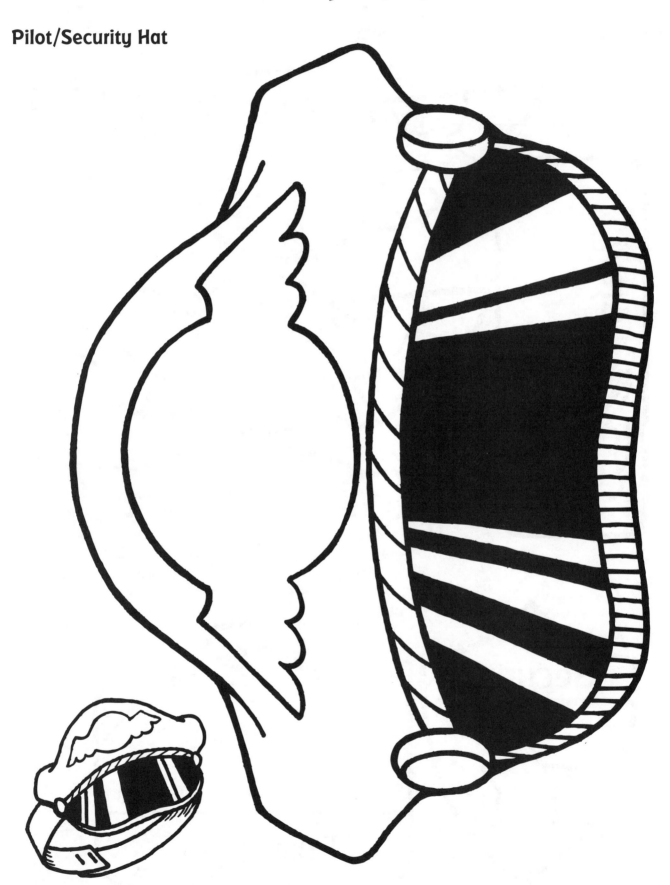

The Airport *(cont.)*

Phase 4: Open the Airport

1. Vote for a favorite destination for each day of the week. Use the destination chart created in Phase 2.

2. Discuss the best way to run the airport and "flights." Form small groups to take turns doing trial runs of the different suggestions. Vote for the best methods.

Student STEM Activities

1. Practice boarding, piloting, serving travelers, and deplaning. Fine-tune an operating system that all can agree upon.
   (*Science/Technology/Engineering/Math*)

2. Figure out staffing and assign roles for the opening. Work out time frames. Create sign-ups.
   —How many ticketing agents will work a shift? TSAs? Baggage handlers?
   —How will pilots and co-pilots take turns? Flight attendants?
   —How many passengers can fly at a time? (*Engineering/Math*)

3. Establish destinations, flight times, and durations (in minutes). Create a Departures chart.
   (*Science/Technology/Engineering/Math*)

4. Check weather conditions for the destination or destinations for the day.
   (*Science/Technology/Math*)

Teacher Support

1. Assist students in constructing a Departures chart. Find each location on a map or a globe.

2. Provide opportunities for research and discussion. Allow time and support for experimentation. Allow an extended period of time for the grand opening of the airport.

3. Help students create a Stand-by list for those children who were not able to make it on the flight they wish. Explain that if they put their name on this list, it means that they will take turns in the order in which their names appear on the list.

4. Film flights and operations for later viewing. Take and post pictures.

Departures		
Monday	New York City	10:00
Tuesday	Washington, D.C.	9:00
Wednesday	Los Angeles	12:00
Thursday	Green Bay	4:00
Friday	Honolulu	7:00

The Airport (*cont.*)

Phase 5: Improve the Airport

1. Discuss what is working well in the airport. Are the flights running smoothly?

2. Analyze what needs fine-tuning.

3. Consider making an air traffic control tower or an airport restaurant. What about night flights? Could flashlights and glow sticks be incorporated?

Student STEM Activities

1. Problem-solve to find better solutions to any difficulties mentioned in the brainstorming sessions.

   —Does the layout of the airport and other airplane areas work? If not, how could it be rearranged?

   —Do the passengers get good service? If not, what would improve the situation?

   (Engineering/Math)

2. Collaborate and implement suggestions for improvement. (***Science/Technology/Engineering/Math***)

3. Enjoy the center. Continue collaborating and improving it. (***Science/Technology/Engineering/Math***)

Teacher Support

1. Consider taking pictures of students and creating "photo identification" for children to present when having their boarding pass verified.

2. Assist with problem solving.

3. Create a graphic organizer to list the responses to the student discussion.

Worked	Needs More Work	Solutions

Notes to Teachers: The airport project can continue for days or weeks, become a permanent fixture, or morph into something else entirely. Student interest will determine its continuing value.

STEM in the Auto Repair Shop

Science

Physics—What makes cars run? What is the difference between a wheel and a tire?

Safety—Why is it so important to follow directions and take safety precautions in an auto repair shop? What can happen if a worker does not?

Chemistry—What will happen when the mechanic's tools are left on the black paper and set out in the sun?

Technology

Internet Research—Find pictures of cars, car engines, and license plates. Search for ideas to arrange and decorate the auto repair shop. Learn about relevant tools and machinery. Find ideas for creating cars and car engines.

Desktop Publishing—Make copies of repair shop interiors, engines, and tools to use for display. Create labels, name tags, and work order sheets. Design advertising flyers or business cards. Create driver's licenses with student photos and design "Free Car Wash" coupons.

Engineering

Drawing—Plan and map the layout for the auto repair shop. Include areas for service and waiting.

Creating Spaces—Arrange a space for the auto repair shop using materials at hand. Create other items as needed using materials collected. Create a lift to service cars.

Designing—Construct cars using cardboard boxes. Design car engines. Make license plates.

Collaborating and Problem Solving—Determine how to set up a mechanic's workstation, who will work it, and who will work as service writers. Determine how many cars to make and how many cars can be serviced in the shop at a given time. Establish when and how the customers can use their free car wash if it is determined that one will be added.

Math

Numbers—Count the number of cars, wheels, doors on a car, numbers on a license plate, etc.

Sequencing—In what order is a car checked for a tune-up? (**Example:** oil–air pressure–tire rotation–engine) What other sequences are part of working in an auto repair shop?

Size and Measurement—Compare sizes of cars and car parts. Measure air pressure and the amount of oil (water) needed for an oil change.

Addition and Subtraction—Compute the cost of services. Add the numbers on the license plates.

Money—Establish prices, compute the amount of a bill, and make change.

Auto Repair Shop Starters

Suggested Props and Materials

○ auto catalogs and magazines

○ Auto Repair Shop Work Order template (page 36)

○ black construction paper

○ cardboard boxes (include an appliance box if possible)

○ clipboards

○ construction paper (black and other colors)

○ creepers

○ Car Engine template (see page 32)

○ funnels

○ keys

○ manipulatives with gear-like parts

○ paper plates (red and yellow)

○ posterboard

○ shoe boxes and small bins

○ steering wheel (real or created)

○ tire gauge

○ tool boxes and tools

○ Velcro

Others

_____

_____

_____

_____

_____

_____

_____

_____

_____

Auto Repair Shop Starters *(cont.)*

Vocabulary

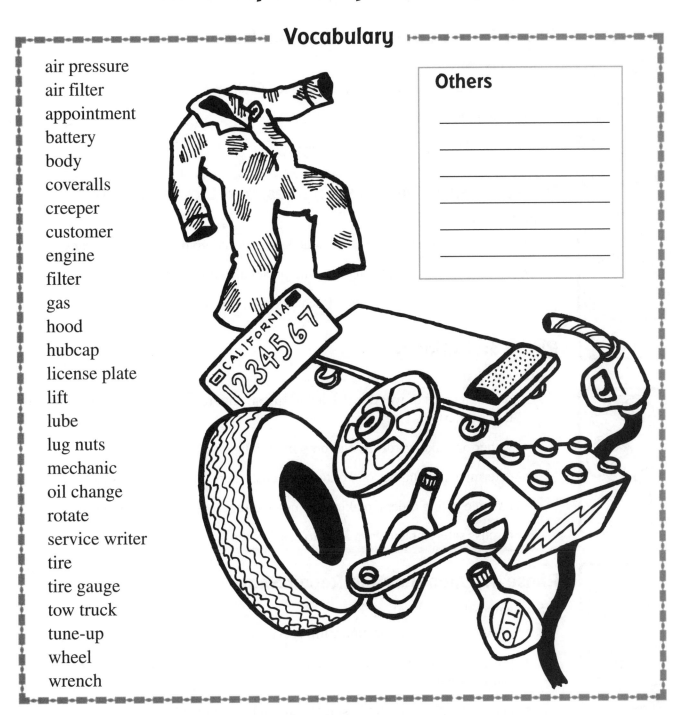

air pressure
air filter
appointment
battery
body
coveralls
creeper
customer
engine
filter
gas
hood
hubcap
license plate
lift
lube
lug nuts
mechanic
oil change
rotate
service writer
tire
tire gauge
tow truck
tune-up
wheel
wrench

Others

_____
_____
_____
_____
_____
_____

Books

We Need Auto Mechanics by Helen Frost
I Want to Be a Mechanic by Dan Liebman
Auto Mechanic by Aileen Weintraub
Auto Mechanics by Tracey Boraas
How Does a Car Work? by Sarah Eason

Others

_____
_____
_____

The Auto Repair Shop Plan

Phase 1: Set Up the Auto Repair Shop

Students will:

- research, design, and set up an auto repair shop

- maintain a word wall

- name the shop and create signage

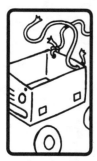

Phase 2: Make Vehicles, Engines, and License Plates

Students will:

- research different makes and models of cars and graph or chart favorites

- create "prop" cars, car engines, and personalized license plates

- print work order sheets and "free car wash" tickets

Phase 3: Define Roles

Students will:

- research types of workers needed to run an auto repair shop and formulate job descriptions

- gather or make wardrobe and prop materials

- determine the number of workers and customers; make sign-up sheets

- practice taking orders, making repairs and tune-ups, and using money

- discuss safety practices in an auto repair shop

Phase 4: Open the Auto Repair Shop

Students will:

- organize mechanics' stations, lift, service areas, and a waiting area.

- practice making repairs, checking and changing oil, air pressure checks, and tire rotations

- open the repair shop for business and implement the plans

Phase 5: Improve the Auto Repair Shop

Students will:

- evaluate what worked and what needs adjusting

- initiate improvements

- enjoy the newly created space and expand and improve as desired

The Auto Repair Shop

Phase 1: Set Up the Auto Repair Shop

1. Let's make an auto repair shop! What do we know about cars and other vehicles? Why would they need to be brought in to a repair shop? What do we need to set one up? What do we have that could be used? What do we need to find and/or borrow?

2. Create webs or lists of ideas and suggestions. Add to these organizational charts as students become more involved in the plan for the auto repair shop.

3. Start a word wall for terms pertinent to the repair shop. Add to it as interest grows.

4. Vote on a name for the class auto repair shop.

Student STEM Activities

1. Research auto repair shops and gather pictures. Share data. Discuss different areas of the shop. Create a sign for the repair shop. (***Technology/Math***)

2. Gather materials and classroom furniture to set up the auto repair shop based on the maps and brainstorming sessions. Determine what is needed, what will fit, and where it should be placed. (***Technology/Engineering/Math***)

3. Collaborate and create mechanics' workstations. Try placing tools on black construction paper and leaving them out in the bright sunlight to create "shadows" on the paper. Then use the paper in the shop to remember where to put tools away. (***Science/Technology/Engineering/Math***)

4. Create a lift. Perhaps taping car engine pictures (or enlarging the template on page 32) to the underside of a table or box would be a possibility. If available, use a creeper to roll underneath and "work on the engine." See the illustration on page 28. Otherwise, slide under the table. (***Technology/Engineering***)

5. Establish a service counter and waiting area. (***Technology/Engineering/Math***)

Teacher Support

1. Listen and record student responses during brainstorming sessions. Offer encouragement and guidance when appropriate.

2. Fill the classroom with related books, word cards, pictures and posters of cars, tools, and engines. Include student contributions as they are created.

3. Create word cards for a pocket chart or a word wall. Keep adding pertinent vocabulary words as they come up. See page 29 for suggestions.

4. Call local auto repair shops for donations (business cards, shirts, work order forms, pictures, posters, etc.) Find out if one will accommodate field trips.

5. Ask parents to donate or gather materials, or to help with cutting or assembly to get the shop started. Invite parents in related industries to come in and share their work experiences.

The Auto Repair Shop *(cont.)*

Car Engine

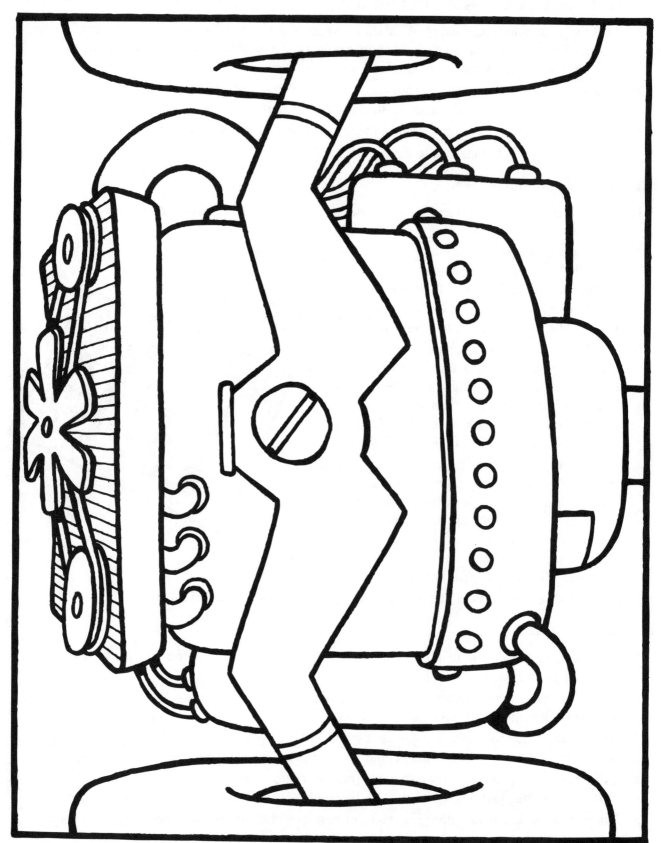

The Auto Repair Shop *(cont.)*

Phase 2: Make Vehicles, Engines, and License Plates

1. Brainstorm a list of favorite types of vehicles (*car, truck, van, jeep*, etc.) and graph them to determine the top four.

2. Plan the repair services the shop will offer. Don't forget the tow truck! Consider some combination services.

3. How can a tow truck be made? What could be used to carry the broken car? (Try a bent hanger duct-taped to a box. See below.)

car	truck	van	jeep
X	X X	X	X
X	X X	X	

Student STEM Activities

1. Create the bodies of the cars and the tow truck using cardboard boxes and other materials. Use paper plates to create the tires and attach them to the car with Velcro. This will allow for easy "tire rotation." *(Technology/Engineering/Math)*

2. Find out about air pressure in tires and why it is important to have the correct amount of air in tires. Find out how and why tires are rotated in vehicles. *(Science/Technology/Engineering/Math)*

3. Discover how and why oil is changed. *(Science/Technology/Math)*

4. Design engine replicas using manipulatives such as connecting blocks, links, gears, etc., and art supplies and recycled materials (plastic bottle caps, lids). *(Engineering)*

5. Research the origin of license plates and why they are used. Create personalized license plates. Each student can attach his or her plate to the back of the car with Velcro when it his or her turn to drive the car. *(Technology/Engineering)*

Teacher Support

1. Enlist parent help in creating the vehicles and engines.

2. Provide opportunities for students to look at examples of engines to help them design their own.

3. Obtain shoebox-sized boxes to create tool boxes and provide bins for storing tools and equipment.

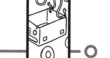

The Auto Repair Shop *(cont.)*

Make a Car

1. Start a collection of copy paper-sized boxes and recycled materials such as plastic lids, tops, small containers, Velcro, foil, ribbon or twine, and other art materials if available.

2. Cut the bottom out of a box, or make large enough holes for students to fit legs through to wear a box around the midsection. If desired, paint the boxes.

3. Add "suspenders" using, twine, ribbon, or elastic.

4. Use small red or yellow paper plates or plastic lids for headlights and taillights.

5. Cover pieces of cardboard with foil to make grills and bumpers.

6. Attach Velcro to the sides of boxes and the backs of large paper plates to make tires that can be changed or rotated. Consider designing fancy rims!

Make Yarn and Clothespin Jumper Cables

The Auto Repair Shop *(cont.)*

Phase 3: Define Roles

1. Construction is underway and the auto repair shop needs a staff and customers. Let's brainstorm different jobs and create a list of possible workers.

2. Discuss each job and list the responsibilities attached to it. What skills would each worker need to be successful? Will the workers dealing with customers have certain things to say? If so, plan dialogue.

3. Figure out wardrobe items or props for each job. Find them in the classroom, borrow them, or make them.

4. Discuss safety in the Auto Repair Shop and when towing cars.

Student STEM Activities

1. Research auto repair shop jobs and then share data. Collect and display pictures. *(Technology)*

2. Gather materials to create and store the props and wardrobe items for each position. Improvise to create additional props. Perhaps students could create or decorate vests made from paper grocery bags with holes cut for necks and arms. Use your imaginations! *(Science/Technology/Engineering/Math)*

3. Create labels or name tags for each position. Consider making time sheets for workers and an appointment book and sign-up sheets to use with customers. Make service order sheets for technicians or copy the one on page 36. *(Technology/Engineering)*

4. Act out the roles of the mechanics, service writers, and tow-truck drivers. Note how often math and science are used in an auto repair shop. *(Science/Technology/Engineering/Math)*

5. Practice using money and a calculator, cash register, or moneybox. *(Technology/Math)*

Teacher Support

1. Review the list of jobs and their responsibilities, and provide wardrobe or prop ideas. Suggest scenarios like a car with a tire that fell off or an engine that won't start.

2. Model the role of the service writer. Demonstrate how to take an order and bring it to the mechanic. Use one of the sample work order sheets provided until students are comfortable creating their own.

3. Discuss the importance of listening to the customers, asking good questions, and writing orders clearly. Good service and manners are important!

4. Review safety procedures.

Auto Repair Shop Work Order

Customer: _____

Car Type

Oil Change

[ ]

Check Air in Tires

[ ]

Rotate Tires

[ ]

Check Engine

[ ]

Other:

The Auto Repair Shop *(cont.)*

Phase 4: Open the Auto Repair Shop

1. Discuss the best way to service each car and the services (oil change, tire rotation, brakes, engine repair) to be provided.

2. Determine if there should be more than one mechanic on duty. Should cars be serviced one at a time, or should different people have different tasks for each car?

3. Vote for the best methods to implement and open for business. Other methods may be implemented at a later date.

Student STEM Activities

1. Document the servicing process. Post pictures or posters of the process or make a "service manual." *(Science/Technology/Engineering)*

2. Take turns servicing vehicles in the auto repair shop. Be aware that changes and adjustments might be needed. If more than one strong suggestion has been made, form small groups to take turns doing trial runs of the different suggestions. *(Science/Engineering/Math)*

3. Figure out staffing and routines and assign roles for the opening.

   —How many mechanics will work a shift? Who will work on engines, tires, brakes, etc.?

   —How will the service counter be managed?

   —How many customers can be serviced at a time? *(Technology/Math)*

4. Work out time frames. Create sign-ups, work order sheets, or "Free Car Wash" tickets.

   —How long will the auto repair shop be open each day?

   —How long will "shifts" be?

   (Technology/Math)

Teacher Support

1. Listen to student brainstorming sessions. Provide guidance when needed.

2. Provide opportunities for research and discussion. Allow time and support for experimentation. Allow an extended period of time for the opening of the auto repair shop.

3. Encourage students to try different methods of repair. Review the concept of *trial and error* if necessary, and provide time for students to explore different options.

4. Film or photograph the auto repair shop in operation to share with students and parents.

The Auto Repair Shop *(cont.)*

Phase 5: Improve the Auto Repair Shop

1. Discuss what is working well.

2. Analyze what needs fine-tuning.

3. Consider additions like a gas station or a car wash.

Note: A simple car wash can be created by cutting large front and back openings in an appliance box. Hang strips of plastic trash bags or paper over each opening. Smaller boxes can be used to create gas pumps. Glue on recycled caps for gauges and add some tubing or short sections of a garden hose.

Student STEM Activities

1. Problem-solve to find better solutions to any difficulties mentioned in the brainstorming sessions.

    —Does the layout of the auto repair shop and the mechanic's area work? If not, how could it be rearranged?

    —Does the repair plan work? If not, what needs to be adjusted and why?

    —Do the customers get speedy service? If not, what would improve the situation?
    (Science/Technology/Engineering/Math)

2. Collaborate and implement suggestions for improving the different areas in the shop.
    (Science/Technology/Engineering/Math)

3. Enjoy the Auto Repair Shop. Continue collaborating and improving it.
    (Science/Technology/Engineering/Math)

Teacher Support

1. Create a graphic organizer to list the responses to the student discussion and assist with problem solving for issues that arose.

Worked	Needs More Work	Solutions

Notes to Teachers: The auto repair shop project can continue for days or weeks, become a permanent fixture, or morph into something else entirely. Student interest will determine its continuing value. The use of license plates can lend itself to a literacy center as well.

STEM in the Bowling Alley

cience

Physics—Find out why bowling pins are arranged in a triangle. What are bowling pins made of? Why are the balls so heavy? What is the best way to roll the ball? How can a bowling ball return be constructed in order for the ball to make it back to the bowler?

Safety—Discuss why it is important to take turns at the bowling alley. What role do workers play in ensuring safety? Why are special shoes required? How are repairs made?

echnology

Internet Research—Find examples of bowling alley interiors. Learn about how specific machines are used within the bowling alley. How are pins set up?

Desktop Publishing—Make copies of score sheets and create labels to use for display or reference. Create name tags and design advertising flyers or a field trip announcement.

Calculators—Use calculators to tally "pins up" scores in the Calculation Station.

ngineering

Drawing—Plan and map the layout for the bowling alley. Include areas for service, bowling, waiting, and scoring.

Creating Spaces—Arrange the bowling alley using materials at hand and create other items as needed. Designate an area where an overhead will project scores on a wall or other area.

Designing—Make a bowling ball return, lanes, and a space for pinsetters.

Collaborating and Problem Solving—Determine how the counter area and Calculation Station should be set up and who will work it. Determine a scorekeeping system and one for setting pins. Establish rules for taking turns, what to do when finished bowling, and what to do while waiting for a turn.

ath

Numbers—Count the number of pins up and pins down to establish awareness of combinations of ten. Count the number of strikes. Keep track of the number of patrons.

Sequencing— Practice arranging 10 pins. Arrange scores in order from lowest to highest.

Size and Measurement—Focus on odd or even and greater than or less than. Weigh and measure a real bowling ball and compare its measurement to students and items in the room.

Addition and Subtraction—Add and subtract numbers of pins. Calculate and write scores.

Money—Establish prices, compute the amount of fees, and practice making change.

Market Research—Chart and graph bowling scores to find the highest, the lowest, and the most frequent scores. Track the number of customers. Determine the most popular ball colors, shoes, etc. Do more students prefer to play five frames or 10 frames?

Bowling Alley Starters

Suggested Props and Materials

- ◯ baby wipes
- ◯ bowling scores template (page 47)
- ◯ calculators for tabulating scores
- ◯ cash registers and play money
- ◯ masking tape
- ◯ overhead projectors or interactive whiteboard
- ◯ plastic bowling balls
- ◯ plastic bowling pins
- ◯ real bowling ball and pin (optional)
- ◯ scale (to measure a bowling ball)
- ◯ Score Cards templates (pages 45 and 46)
- ◯ sentence strips for mounting names on the High Score wall
- ◯ washable markers
- ◯ wooden blocks or other material to create bowling lanes

Others

_____

_____

_____

_____

_____

Vocabulary

bumpers	gutter	return	split
frame	lane	scorekeeper	strike
foul line	pinsetter	spare	turkey

Others _____ _____ _____

Books

Curious George Goes Bowling by H.A. Rey

I Can Bowl by Edana Eckart

I Can Bowl! by Linda Johns

Bowling in Action by John Crossingham

Bowling for Beginners: Simple Steps to Strikes & Spares by Don Nace

Others

_____

_____

_____

The Bowling Alley Plan

Phase 1: Set Up the Bowling Alley

Students will:

- research the origins of the game of bowling and graph personal experiences—who has or has not been bowling, gotten a strike, or used bumpers?
- research and design a bowling alley
- gather materials and furnishings and plan areas for bowling lanes, pin resetting, and bowling ball returns
- prepare areas for service, waiting, calculating scores, and viewing scores
- maintain a word wall
- vote on a name for the bowling alley and create signage

Phase 2: Create Lanes, Ball Returns, and Pin-Reset Areas

Students will:

- learn what real bowling balls and pins are made of and determine why the balls need to be so heavy and the pins arranged as they are
- construct a bowling ball return
- create score sheets; determine costs for bowling
- make and maintain a high score wall and create awards or trophies

Phase 3: Define Roles

Students will:

- research types of workers needed to run a bowling alley
- formulate job descriptions (include hygiene discussion)
- gather or make wardrobe items and prop materials
- determine the number of workers and customers; make sign-ups
- practice waiting on bowlers, calculating scores, and using money and calculators

Phase 4: Open the Bowling Alley

Students will:

- decide how to sign up to bowl and where others will wait for an open lane
- practice a trial run with bowlers and workers, and adjust as needed
- open the bowling alley for business

Phase 5: Improve the Bowling Alley

Students will:

- discuss what they are enjoying about the bowling alley, what is working, and what needs adjusting
- initiate improvements based on discussions and research
- enjoy the newly created space and expand and improve as desired

The Bowling Alley

Phase 1: Set Up the Bowling Alley

1. Start a discussion with students. What do we know about bowling and bowling alleys? Who's been bowling? What kinds of things do we need in order to create a bowling alley? What do we have that could be used? What do we need to find and/or borrow?

2. Create lists of ideas and suggestions. Add to these organizational charts as they become more involved in the planning.

3. If possible, examine a real bowling ball. How much does it weigh? More or less than _____.

4. Create a word wall for terms pertinent to the bowling alley.

5. Vote on a name for the class bowling alley.

Student STEM Activities

1. Research bowling and bowling alleys and provide pictures when possible. Share data and map out a plan for the space. Create a sign for the bowling alley. (***Technology/Engineering***)

2. Gather materials and classroom furniture to set up the bowling alley based on the research findings, brainstorming sessions, and maps. Determine what is needed, what will fit, and where it will go. (***Science/Technology/Engineering/Math***)

3. Collaborate and plan the bowling lanes and bowling ball returns, and where pinsetters will be stationed. (***Science/Technology/Engineering/Math***)

4. Set up a front counter, a waiting area, and an area for calculating bowling scores. Stock the Calculation Station area with laminated recording sheets, wipes, pencils, and calculators. (***Technology/Engineering/Math***)

5. Weigh and measure a real bowling ball. Find other things that weigh more or less than the ball and create a chart. (***Science/Technology/Math***)

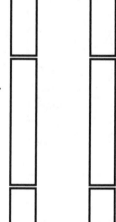

Teacher Support

1. Record student responses during brainstorming sessions. Graph experiences— Who has been bowling; who has not? With bumpers or without? Offer encouragement and provide reasonable amounts of research and planning time.

2. Fill the classroom with related books, word cards, sample score sheets, pictures, and posters. Include student contributions as they are created.

3. Create word cards for a pocket chart or a word wall. Continue to add relevant vocabulary words as suggested. (See page 40 for suggestions.)

4. Call local bowling alleys for donations (shirts, score sheets, old trophies). Ask if they will accommodate a field trip.

5. Ask parents to help with materials, or to help with assembly or construction to get the bowling alley started. Invite parents to share their experiences if they have been in leagues, won trophies, coached, or worked at an alley.

The Bowling Alley *(cont.)*

Phase 2: Create Lanes, Ball Returns, and Pin-Reset Areas

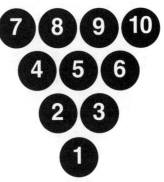

1. Discuss how many lanes will fit, including bowling ball returns. (**Note:** If two lanes are to be created, the bowling ball return can be shared to save space. See the illustration below.)

2. If possible, compare real pins to the plastic classroom set. Discuss the traditional 10-pin set-up and why it works in the triangular format.

3. Figure out how to set up pin-reset areas. Should there be markers on the floor?

Student STEM Activities

1. Research bowling pin set ups and arrange the pins and the pinsetter area. Find out what bowling balls are made of and why they are so heavy. (***Science/Technology/Engineering/Math***)

2. Construct lanes with a foul line, a pin resetting area, and a bowling ball return. Lanes can be made using blocks, 2 x 4s, PVC pipes, etc. (***Engineering/Math***)

3. Create personal bowling score sheets or use the sheets provided (pages 45 and 46). When complete, these can be taken home to share and to generate more interest in the center. (***Technology/Math***)

4. Devise a wall for high scores. (***Engineering/Math***)

5. Decide the prices for bowling. (***Math***)

Teacher Support

1. Explain the concept of trial and error and provide time for students to explore different options, such as where the foul line is placed, the length of the lanes, and the space between the pins. Provide guidance when needed. Other students can be working on signage and other ideas mentioned during brainstorming.

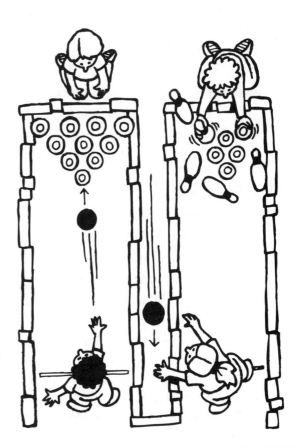

2. Assist with lane set-up and with pin arrangements until students are comfortable.

3. Have the "_____ Score" transparencies, (pages 45 and 46), washable markers, and baby wipes available for calculation area.

4. Enlist parent help in constructing more permanent lanes using 2 x 4s or loaning other items to enhance the area.

5. Provide opportunities for students in decorating the area or for making signs.

The Bowling Alley *(cont.)*

Phase 3: Define Roles

1. Construction is underway and the bowling alley needs a staff and bowlers. Brainstorm different bowling alley jobs and create a list of possible workers.

2. Discuss each job and its responsibilities. What skills would each worker need to be successful? Will the scorekeeper use a calculator or will adult assistance be needed? How do you bowl?

3. Figure out wardrobe items or props for each job and for bowlers.

4. Discuss proper bowling etiquette, including turn-taking, appropriate noise and voice levels, how to roll the ball, etc. Include a discussion of hygiene—cleaning balls, pins, etc.

Student STEM Activities

1. Research jobs needed to make a bowling alley successful. Share data and collect and display appropriate pictures. (***Technology/Engineering***)

2. Gather materials to create and store the props and wardrobe items for each position. Improvise and create additional props needed using classroom materials and imagination! (***Science/Technology/Engineering/Math***)

3. Create labels or name tags for each position. Consider making time sheets for pinsetters, counter personnel, ball "returners," and scorekeepers. Create reservations/sign-in sheets for bowlers. (***Technology/Math***)

4. Practice keeping score and using the High Score wall. Use money, a cash register, and the ball returns. (***Science/Technology/Math***)

5. Practice bowling with proper form and setting pins accurately. Consider having the physical education teacher or someone from your local bowling alley come in and demonstrate! (***Science/Technology/Engineering/Math***)

Teacher Support

1. Review the list of jobs and their responsibilities. Provide name tags or bowling shirts, or make other prop and wardrobe suggestions based on materials available.

2. Model the role of the counter person. Demonstrate how to assign lanes to bowlers based on availability. Stress that good service is important!

3. Demonstrate how to bowl and how to keep score using the score sheets. Discuss the High Score wall. Review the sample score sheets and directions on pages 45–47. Explain that each bowler will have a scorekeeper who marks pins left up and pins that went down. (Scoring is a bit different than scoring at an actual bowling alley. The score sheets were designed to facilitate taking turns and are not identical to actual bowling frames. Bowlers have the option to bowl five or 10 times, depending on the scorecard used.) When the turn is finished, the bowler will bring the transparency to the Calculation Station and fill out his or her personal score card to post or take home.

The Bowling Alley *(cont.)*

Directions: Copy the score sheets onto transparencies or laminate them to be used in the bowling alley. Students should fill in their names and the scorekeeper will fill in the numbers.

Scoring

Step 1—Bowler rolls the ball and counts how many pins are knocked down and how many remain standing.

Step 2—Bowler reports findings to scorekeeper who records the "pins down" and "pins up" on the recording sheet while the pinsetter resets the pins.

Step 3—Bowler repeats steps 1 and 2 until all "frames" have been bowled.

Step 4—Bowler takes score sheet to the calculation station where a student with a calculator or an adult helps tally the scores.

Step 5—Bowler fills in score on a certificate (page 47) and posts it or takes it home to share with family. All scores are reported to the person in charge of the High Score wall.

_____'s SCORE

_____ ↑ + _____ ↓ = 10

_____ ↑ + _____ ↓ = 10

_____ ↑ + _____ ↓ = 10

_____ ↑ + _____ ↓ = 10

_____ ↑ + _____ ↓ = 10

_____'s SCORE

_____ ↑   +   _____ ↓   =   10

_____ ↑   +   _____ ↓   =   10

_____ ↑   +   _____ ↓   =   10

_____ ↑   +   _____ ↓   =   10

_____ ↑   +   _____ ↓   =   10

_____ ↑   +   _____ ↓   =   10

_____ ↑   +   _____ ↓   =   10

_____ ↑   +   _____ ↓   =   10

_____ ↑   +   _____ ↓   =   10

_____ ↑   +   _____ ↓   =   10

MY BOWLING SCORE WAS _____

Name: _____

MY BOWLING SCORE WAS _____

Name: _____

The Bowling Alley *(cont.)*

Phase 4: Open the Bowling Alley

1. Discuss the best way to run the bowling alley.

2. If more than one strong suggestion has been made, form small groups to take turns doing trial runs of the different suggestions.

3. Vote for the best method to run the bowling alley and open for business.

Student STEM Activities

1. Take turns with the various bowling alley jobs and/or plans for running the alley. (*Science/Technology/Engineering/Math*)

2. Practice and fine-tune a system that all can agree upon. Be aware that, once the bowling alley opens, adjustments might be needed. (*Science/Technology/Engineering/Math*)

3. Figure out staffing and assign roles for the opening. Create sign-up sheets.

   —How do bowlers sign up for a turn?

   —Each bowler will need a pinsetter and a scorekeeper.

   —Will there be a greeter at the front desk to hand out balls?

   —How many customers can bowl at a time? (*Technology/Engineering/Math*)

4. Open for business.

   —How long will the bowling alley be open (class period, all day)?

   —How long will shifts (turns) be? (*Math*)

Teacher Support

1. Listen to student brainstorming sessions. Provide guidance when needed.

2. Provide opportunities for experimentation. Allow an extended period of time for the grand opening of the bowling alley.

3. Take video of bowlers and employees in action. Use the film to improve bowling technique and to highlight examples of gracious turn-taking, service, etc.

4. Demonstrate how to take pictures of each other holding score sheets. These can be printed and displayed in the bowling alley as well as used to create a book. Add sentences to the pictures and display it or place it in the book area for independent reading. Make extra copies of the book to share with your local bowling alley! It becomes good PR for your school, and they may be willing to donate items based on what they see in your photos.

The Bowling Alley (cont.)

Phase 5: Improve the Bowling Alley

1. Discuss what is working well in the bowling alley.

2. Analyze what needs fine-tuning. Are the pins being set up quickly enough? Do we need more workers at each of the stations? How can more bowlers bowl in a certain time period?

3. Consider additions—a snack bar, trophies and a trophy case, perhaps a pro shop.

Student STEM Activities

1. Problem-solve to find better solutions to any difficulties mentioned in the brainstorming sessions. (*Engineering/Math*)

   —Does the layout of the bowling alley and other counter areas work? If not, how could it be rearranged?

   —Do the customers get good service? If not, what would improve the situation?

Worked	Needs More Work	Solutions

2. Collaborate and implement suggestions for improvement. (*Science/Technology/Engineering/Math*)

3. Have students experiment in small groups with different combinations of pin placement. What arrangement makes it most difficult to get a strike? What arrangement is the easiest? (*Science/Engineering/Math*)

4. Enjoy the center. Continue collaborating and improving it. (*Science/Technology/Engineering/Math*)

Teacher Support

1. Create a graphic organizer to list the responses to student discussions.

2. Assist with problem solving.

Note to Teachers: The bowling alley project can continue for days or weeks, be shared with other classes, or morph into something completely different.

STEM in the Flower Shop

cience

Life Science—Talk about flowers. Flowers can start as seeds. Do all seeds look the same? Some flowers start growing as bulbs. How are these different? What do flowers need to grow? Do all flowers grow at the same rate? What can impede the growth of flowers? Do all flowers live for the same amount of time? How do you take care of cut flowers?

echnology

Internet Research—Find information about different kinds of flower seeds, bulbs, flower arrangements, and florist shops. Look for ideas to arrange flowers and to decorate the shop. Find out how flowers get to the florist shop. Learn about relevant tools, such as cash registers, displays, and other possible props.

Desktop Publishing—Print pictures of floral arrangements; make price tags, signage, advertising, coupons, order forms, and delivery or gift cards.

ngineering

Drawing—Plan and map the layout for the florist shop. Include areas for taking orders, creating flower arrangements, and ringing up sales. Don't forget the display areas!

Creating Spaces—Arrange storage, prep, and display areas using available bins, shelves, and tables.

Designing—Make flowers. Make flower arrangements and displays for them. Create signs, cards, and labels.

Collaborating and Problem Solving—Figure out ways to assemble arrangements and display them artfully. Should arrangements be taken apart each day? Discuss the roles and expectations for those working in the flower shop and for the customers.

ath

Numbers—Count the number of petals on a flower, the number of flowers in an order, or the number of arrangements being purchased.

Sequencing— How are flower arrangements put together? (*vase→foam→flowers→greenery*) In what order do the flowers have to be placed to ensure a nice looking arrangement? What system do customers need to follow when filling out their order form?

Size and Measurement—Note the different sizes and shapes of vases and flowers, or the amounts of flowers in different vases or containers. Is the arrangement or flower small, medium, or large?

Addition and Subtraction—Add or subtract numbers of flowers or petals.

Money—Establish prices, compute the amount of a bill, and make change.

Market Research—Chart and graph the colors of flowers in the store. Discuss why a certain color or flower might be more popular than another. Determine the best sellers.

Flower Shop Starters

Suggested Props and Materials

- ◯ baskets
- ◯ bows, ribbon, and other decorative items
- ◯ boxes for displays
- ◯ cash registers and play money
- ◯ coupons and store flyers
- ◯ floral foam
- ◯ Gift Cards for Flowers templates (page 57)
- ◯ paper for making flowers, labels, signs, and tags
- ◯ pictures of flowers and flower arrangements
- ◯ pipe cleaners
- ◯ plastic vases and containers
- ◯ plastic or silk flowers
- ◯ Price List template (page 56)
- ◯ small, live plants
- ◯ tables, chairs, shelving
- ◯ tissue and crepe paper for arrangements

Others

_____
_____
_____
_____
_____
_____
_____
_____
_____

Flower Shop Starters *(cont.)*

Vocabulary

arrangements	corsage	flower	root
artificial	coupon	leaf	sale
boutonniere	delivery	leaves	seed
bulbs	fertilizer	petal	stem
cash and carry	florist	refrigeration	vase
			weed

Others

_____
_____
_____
_____
_____

Books

At the Flower Shop: Learning Simple Division by Forming Equal Groups by Jennifer Nowark

Flowers (Plant Parts) by Vijaya Bodach

The Flower Alphabet Book by Jerry Pallotta

Planting a Rainbow by Lois Ehlert

Others

_____
_____
_____

The Flower Shop Plan

Phase 1: Set Up the Flower Shop

Students will:

- graph experiences with flowers (Examples: Have you ever grown flowers? Have you sent or received flowers? Which do you like better—real or artificial flowers, and why?)
- research and design a flower shop
- obtain boxes, vases, and other materials
- create areas for taking orders, selling flowers, and making arrangements
- maintain a word wall
- vote on a name for the flower shop and create signage

Phase 2: Make Floral Arrangements

Students will:

- make flowers or arrange collected flowers in different containers
- determine prices for flowers, bouquets, and arrangements
- create and maintain departments within the flower shop
- make order forms, gift cards, and a book showing the arrangements

Phase 3: Define Roles

Students will:

- research types of workers needed to run a flower shop
- formulate job descriptions and make sign-ups
- gather or make wardrobe items and prop materials
- practice taking and preparing orders and using money and cash registers

Phase 4: Open the Flower Shop

Students will:

- decide on how to rotate roles in the store
- perform a trial run with workers and customers and adjust as needed
- open the flower shop for business and implement the planned routines

Phase 5: Improve the Flower Shop

Students will:

- have a class discussion about what works and what needs adjustment
- initiate improvements based on discussions and research
- enjoy the newly created space, and expand and improve as desired

The Flower Shop

Phase 1: Set Up the Flower Shop

1. Start a discussion about flowers. If possible, examine real ones. Why might people want to give or receive flowers? Why are flowers sometimes in refrigerators? Discuss the role flowers play at weddings, anniversaries, proms, and other special occasions.

2. What do we have that could be used to create a flower shop? What do we need to find or borrow? Create lists of ideas and suggestions. Have students add to these organizational charts as they become more involved in the planning.

3. Create a word wall for terms pertinent to the flower shop. Add to it as interest grows.

4. Vote on a name for the class flower shop.

Student STEM Activities

1. Share experiences with flowers and examine real ones. Identify and count stems, leaves, petals, seeds, and roots if looking at plants. (***Science/Technology/Math***)

2. Research flowers and flower shops. Share data and map out a plan for the space. Find or print pictures. Create a sign for the shop. (***Science/Technology/Engineering/Math***)

3. Gather materials and rearrange furniture to set up the flower shop based on the brainstorming sessions and research. Determine what is needed, what will fit, and where it will go. (***Science/Technology/Engineering/Math***)

4. Collaborate, construct, and arrange areas in the flower shop. If live plants are available, place them appropriately. (***Science/Technology/Engineering/Math***)

Teacher Support

1. Listen to and record student responses during the brainstorming sessions.

2. Provide examples of flowers and floral arrangements. Fill the classroom with related books, word cards, sample arrangements, flyers, coupons, pictures, and posters. Include student contributions as they are created.

3. Create word cards for a pocket-chart or a word wall. See page 52 for suggestions. Continue to add relevant vocabulary words as suggested.

4. Call flower shops and floral departments in grocery stores for donations or loans (signs, fixtures, containers). Ask if they will accommodate a field trip.

5. Ask parents to donate or gather materials, such as ribbons, bows, pipe cleaners, and flowers. Ask who could help with assembly or construction to get the flower shop started. Invite parents to come in and share their experiences growing or arranging flowers. See if any have experience working in flower shops.

The Flower Shop *(cont.)*

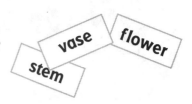

Phase 2: Make Floral Arrangements

1. Discuss what types of flowers will be sold in the shop. Will there be single flowers, flowers sold in bunches, and/or formal arrangements?

2. Figure out what else will be needed to create formal arrangements.

Student STEM Activities

1. Sort flowers by color, size, or type of flower. Display some flowers in the store. Place others on a long table. They can be used for arrangements. (***Science/Engineering/Math***)

2. Create arrangements to sell and to use as store samples. (***Engineering***)

3. Determine prices for arrangements, single flowers, gift items, etc. or use page 56. (***Math***)

4. Create order forms and cards or use the gift card templates provided (page 57). Print copies as needed or use for examples. (***Technology/Engineering/Math***)

5. Take pictures of flowers and arrangements and bind them into a book. This can be used for customers to see examples when placing their orders. Add captions and prices to the pictures and share the book with parents. Later, place *The _____ Flower Shop* book in the reading area. (***Technology/Math***)

   Optional: Make paper flowers. To get started, try the ideas and directions provided on pages 58 and 59 for different types of flowers. (***Science/Technology/Engineering/Math***)

Teacher Support

1. Demonstrate how to create an arrangement using a container or vase, floral foam, flowers, and greenery. Focus on the numbers of flowers used and the colors and sizes of flowers and vases.

2. Provide opportunities for students to search online for pictures of flowers and to look in magazines and seed catalogs. These can be used to decorate the flower shop, to embellish signs and labels, or for arrangement ideas.

3. Encourage students to draw or make flowers with petals, centers (seeds), stems, and leaves.

The Flower Shop *(cont.)*

Price List

1 Flower		$1.00
3 Flowers		$3.00
6 Flowers		$6.00
Dozen Flowers		$12.00
Small Arrangement		$8.00
Large Arrangement		$10.00

The Flower Shop (cont.)

Gift Cards for Flowers

The Flower Shop *(cont.)*

Making Flower #1

Materials: construction paper in a variety of colors, green chenille sticks, scissors

Directions for the Teacher: Make multiple copies of the patterns on different colored sheets of paper. Sort the patterns into three groups—small petals, medium petals, and large petals. Each group should have a variety of color choices. If appropriate, punch holes in the center of each pattern piece. Allow room for creativity. These patterns are templates to get students started.

Making the Flower

1. For each flower, choose a small, medium, and large pattern and a green chenille stick. The patterns can be the same color, or different.

2. Stack the patterns with the largest one on the bottom. Roll one end of a chenille stick (the stem) around a pencil to create a loop (the center of the flower).

3. Push the other end of the chenille stick through the small, medium, and large patterns (in that order).

4. Use a bit of glue to add green construction-paper leaves, if desired.

Patterns

The Flower Shop *(cont.)*

Making Flower #2

Materials: construction paper—2 or more colors, green chenille sticks, scissors, glue; seeds optional

Directions for the Teacher: Prepare two 3.5" circles and six to eight 1" x 4.5" strips (per child) ahead of time to allow students more time to assemble the flowers. Allow room for creativity and adjust sizes as needed. These patterns are merely templates to get students started.

1 Choose two circles and 6–8 strips.

2 Lay one of the circles on a flat surface and cover it with glue.

3 Arrange strips around the circle. About ¼ to ½ inch should be in the glue.

4 Lay the end of a green chenelle stick in the glue.

5 Cover the attached strip ends with a bit more glue and fold the strips over to form loops.

6 Cover the assembly with the second circle, and allow it to dry.

Optional: Add seeds to the center on top.

The Flower Shop *(cont.)*

Phase 3: Define Roles

1. The flower shop needs a staff and customers. Brainstorm different jobs and create a list of possible workers.

2. Discuss each job and list the responsibilities attached to it. What skills would each worker need? What different skills might an arranger need than a counter person? a delivery person?

3. Figure out wardrobe items or props for each job.

Student STEM Activities

1. Research flower shop jobs, share data, and collect and display pictures of house plants, flowers, and flower arrangements. (*Science/Technology/Engineering*)

2. Find wardrobe items in the classroom, borrow them, or make them. Design labels or name tags for each position. Consider making time sheets for workers. (*Technology/Engineering/Math*)

3. Dramatize different roles within the store. Practice taking orders and arranging flowers. Who takes care of the flowers and displays? (*Science/Technology/Engineering/Math*)

4. Note how often math is used when stocking or arranging flowers. Practice using money and a cash register or moneybox. (*Math*)

Teacher Support

1. Review the list of jobs and their responsibilities and provide wardrobe or prop ideas. Consider name tags or smocks, or make other suggestions based on materials available.

2. Model the role of the counter person and how to take an order.

3. Review the responsibilities of a flower arranger. Emphasize the importance of following the sequence (*container* ➙ *flowers* ➙ *greens*) when making an arrangement to meet the customer's specifications.

4. Build upon student discoveries and encourage further study. Video tape the floral shop in action. It is fun to watch and can be used to focus on improving customer relations or other skills.

5. Provide a list of things people may write on the floral cards. (See page 57.) Display the list in the shop for those children who may want to copy. Other children may choose to use inventive spelling.

The Flower Shop (cont.)

Phase 4: Open the Flower Shop

1. Discuss the best way to run the flower shop so things run smoothly.
2. Make a list of all available jobs in the store.
3. Vote for the best methods to implement ideas and open for business.

Student STEM Activities

1. Practice and fine-tune taking orders, flower arranging, and flower making. Care for live plants in the shop. (***Science/Engineering***)

2. Figure out staffing and assign roles for the opening. Create sign-up sheets.

   —How many flower arrangers will work a shift?

   —Will there be delivery persons? Order takers?

   —How long will the flower shop be opened (class period, all day)?

   —How long will shifts (turns) be?

   —Should there be a customer limit in the shop at one time? (***Technology/Engineering/Math***)

3. Document the flower-arranging or flower-making process. Post pictures of the sequences or share videos. (***Technology/Engineering/Math***)

4. Open for business. (***Science/Technology/Engineering/Math***)

Teacher Support

1. Provide opportunities for research and discussion. Allow time and support for experimentation. Allow an extended period of time for the grand opening of the flower shop.

2. Explain the concept of *trial and error* and provide time for students to explore different options. If the first plans voted on do not work, suggest going back and trying other suggestions.

The Flower Shop *(cont.)*

Phase 5: Improve the Flower Shop

1. Discuss what is selling well in the shop.

2. Analyze what needs fine-tuning. Are more flowers or containers needed? More arrangers? Do plants need more care?

3. Consider additions such as wreaths, corsages and boutonnieres, a delivery service, a "refrigeration" area, or additional stock items.

Student STEM Activities

1. Problem solve to find better solutions to any difficulties mentioned in the brainstorming sessions. Does the layout of the store counter and display areas work? If not, how could it be rearranged? Should more flowers be made? Do the customers get good service? If not, what would improve the situation? (***Engineering/Math***)

2. Collaborate and implement suggestions for improvement. (***Science/Technology/Engineering/Math***)

3. Enjoy the center. Continue collaborating and improving it. (***Science/Technology/Engineering/Math***)

Teacher Support

1. Create a graphic organizer to list the responses to the student discussion.

2. Assist with problem solving.

Supplemental Activities

1. Take the children on a nature walk to observe or gather flowers. Take pictures of the flowers and match them to pictures in books. (***Science/Technology***)

2. Consider growing flowers with your students. Select seeds that are quick germinators, such as marigolds, zinnias, snapdragons, or alyssum. Share different types of flower seeds and the matching picture of the flower that will eventually grow. (***Science/Math***)

3. Plant pairs of flowers but apply variables to only one of the matching plants, such as eliminating light or using a liquid other than water for moisture. Record the results. (***Science/Technology/Engineering/Math***)

4. Grow a flower garden at your school. Keep track of growth from seed to flower. Later, flowers can be donated to a nursing home or given as gifts to special helpers in the school or your classroom. (***Science/Technology/Engineering/Math***)

Note to Teachers: This project can continue for days or weeks, be shared with other classes, or morph into something completely different. Student interest will determine its continuing value.

STEM in the Grocery Store

 ## science

Nutrition and Health—Determine where different foods and food products come from. Are they grown or manufactured? How does the food need to be stored to remain fresh? Why do some things need to be refrigerated?

Chemistry/Cooking—What kinds of dishes can be prepared with the foods in the store? Can they be eaten alone? Are all items in a grocery store edible?

Hygiene and Safety—Why is it important to keep a store and things in a store clean? Why do workers have to make sure things are put away properly?

 ## technology

Internet Research—Find information about the different sections of a grocery store. Do they all look the same? Do some have bakeries or delis? Do some have self check-outs? Look for ideas to arrange and decorate the store. Learn about relevant tools such as scales, cash registers, grocery carts, and other possible props.

Desktop Publishing—Make copies of price tags, signage, advertising, coupons, grocery lists, and name tags.

 ## engineering

Drawing—Plan and map out the layout for the grocery store. Include areas for the different departments, cart returns, and the checkout stand(s).

Creating Spaces—Arrange the grocery store using classroom furniture, boxes, and other materials at hand. A longer table works well for the checkout stand.

Designing—Use boxes, baskets, etc. to create a produce section. Consider using larger or longer boxes to create refrigerated areas. A black piece of paper with lines on it can be attached to a longer table to represent a conveyor belt for the check-out station. (See The Airport, page 19, for a conveyor belt.) Don't forget areas for carts and for bagging groceries.

Collaborating and Problem Solving—What is the best way to stack cans and boxes? Where will the groceries go once a shopper has finished shopping? How will the purchases be put back on the shelves?

 ## math

Numbers—Count the number of workers needed, the number of patrons, the amount of items on a grocery list, the number of items being purchased, and the number of departments.

Sequencing—What is the order that customers need to follow when shopping (list, shop, pay, carry out)? Are there sequences for stocking shelves, ringing up orders, preparing food at a deli or bakery counter?

Size and Measurement—Compare the amount of items–greater than or less than; note sizes of items–small, medium, large, extra large; weigh and compare items–heavy, light.

Addition and Subtraction—Add or subtract the number of items written on the grocery list or in the basket.

Money—Establish prices, compute the amount of a bill, and make change for the customer.

Market Research—Chart and graph the items that have been sold the most or the least.

Grocery Store Starters

Suggested Props and Materials

- ◯ baskets, bins, and boxes for displays
- ◯ cash registers, calculators, and play money
- ◯ chairs, tables, and shelving
- ◯ child-sized grocery carts
- ◯ child-sized refrigerator
- ◯ coupons and store flyers
- ◯ department labels templates (page 67)
- ◯ empty food boxes, cans, and containers
- ◯ labels for recording weights and to create UPC labels
- ◯ paper for grocery lists, labels, signs, and tags
- ◯ play food
- ◯ purses and wallets
- ◯ scales for weighing produce, meat, and fish
- ◯ shopping bags (reusable and paper or plastic)
- ◯ Shopping List templates (page 69)

Other

_____

_____

_____

_____

_____

Vocabulary

bagger	coupon	manager	sell	supermarket
bakery	dairy	meat	scale	truck
butcher	deli	package	scanner	UPC code
buy	florist	produce	shelves	vegetable
can	freezer	refrigeration	stock	
checker	fruit	sale	stocker	

Others

_____

_____

Books

Grocery Store by Angela Leeper

Working at a Grocery Store by Katie Marsico

What Happens at a Supermarket? by Amy Hutchings

A Visit to the Supermarket by B.A. Hoena

Out and About at the Supermarket by Kitty Shea

Others

_____

_____

_____

The Grocery Store Plan

Phase 1: Set Up the Grocery Store

Students will:

- discuss (and research) different types of grocery stores including a chain store, a "big box" store, a "mom and pop" store, and an express store
- map out and design the class store including weighing stations, service counter space, areas for merchandise within the grocery store, and cart/basket returns
- create different departments such as a bakery, a deli, the produce section, the meat section, or a refrigerated area, depending on the materials
- establish a word wall
- name the store and create signage for the store and the sections within

Phase 2: Create the Check-out and "Returns" Areas

Students will:

- share experiences with grocery shopping
- construct a check-out area with a conveyor belt, cash register, and a bagging station
- figure out what to do with all the food once the shopper leaves the store—who puts it back?
- practice using the cash registers, money, and calculators
- graph the types of bags used for shopping—*paper, plastic,* or *reusable*

Phase 3: Define Roles

Students will:

- research types of workers needed to run a grocery store
- formulate job descriptions
- gather items or make wardrobe items and prop materials
- practice making shopping lists
- try being a shopper and a worker

Phase 4: Open the Grocery Store

Students will:

- determine the number of workers for each section of the store (if any) and the number of customers who can shop at a given time
- practice shopping and purchasing items to determine if there are enough workers and adjust as needed
- open the grocery store for business and implement the plans

Phase 5: Improve the Grocery Store

Students will:

- discuss what is working and what needs adjusting in the store
- initiate improvements based on discussions and research
- enjoy the newly created space and expand and improve as desired

The Grocery Store

Phase 1: Set Up the Grocery Store

1. What do we know about different kinds of grocery stores? What do we need to create one? What do we have that could be used? What do we need to make or borrow?
2. Create lists and organizational charts as interest in the grocery store grows.
3. Start a list of words pertinent to the grocery store.
4. Vote on a name for the store.

Grocery Words	
shop	buy
sort	sell

Student STEM Activities

1. Research groceries and grocery stores. Discuss what goes in the dairy section, in produce, etc. Find or print pictures of products to use for display and pricing. Share data. Embellish the "department" labels provided (page 67) with pictures to get started. Create a sign for the store. *(Science/Technology/Engineering/Math)*
2. Gather materials and classroom furniture to set up the grocery store based on the maps and brainstorming sessions. Collaborate and determine what is needed for each area. Fill food boxes and containers with crumpled scrap paper, beans, or rice, and tape them closed. *(Science/Technology/Engineering/Math)*

3. Discuss which of the collected food items, if real, would need to be refrigerated and why. Arrange areas that will work for "refrigerated" items. **Hints:** A refrigerator box might make a wonderful cooler area! Longer boxes that are filled with packing peanuts can be made to resemble frozen food areas. *(Science/Technology/Engineering/Math)*
4. Figure out ways to display boxed or canned items, and create deli or bakery cases. **Hint:** Boxes might be painted and placed on their sides to create shelving and cases. *(Science/Technology/Engineering/Math)*

Teacher Support

1. Listen and record student responses during the brainstorming sessions. Offer encouragement and provide reasonable amounts of time for research, planning, and creating.
2. Fill the classroom with related books, sample grocery lists, flyers and coupons, Daily Special reminders, pictures, and posters. Include student contributions as they are created.
3. Create word cards for a pocket-chart or a word wall. (See page 64.) Continue to add relevant vocabulary words when appropriate.
4. Call local grocery stores for donations or loans (carts, signs, fixtures, containers, boxes). Find out if they will accommodate field trips.
5. Ask parents to save empty food containers like cereal boxes or detergent containers or to loan other items to enhance the grocery store. Invite parents to come in and share their experiences if they work or have worked at a grocery store.

The Grocery Store *(cont.)*

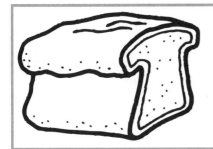  **Bakery**

  **Dairy**

 **Detergent**

 **Flowers**

 **Produce**

 **Deli**  **Meat**

©*Teacher Created Resources*   *#3024 Project-Based Activities for STEM*

The Grocery Store (cont.)

Phase 2: Create the Check-Out and "Returns" Areas

1. Discuss shopping at the grocery store. Do students help make shopping lists? Find items in the store? Push the cart? Place things on the check-out belt? Put things away at home?

2. What happens when it is time to pay for groceries? What is the sequence?

3. How are groceries paid for? (cash, check, credit card, other)

4. Graph the kinds of bags students' families use when shopping—paper, plastic, or reusable.

Student STEM Activities

1. Organize a check-out station with an area for the checker and a cash register, a "conveyor belt" for purchases, and room for a bagger and bags. (*Science/Technology/Engineering/Math*)

2. Construct an area for a cart/basket return. Also decide what to do once a student has finished shopping. Where will the "purchased" food and grocery items go? Should there be a special job for a "re-stocker"? (*Science/Technology/Engineering/Math*)

3. Design shopping lists or use the ones on page 69. Print copies as needed. If appropriate, vote on how many items need to be on a list before a shopper can enter a store. (*Technology/Math*)

4. Decide upon prices for items and on how many items can be purchased at a time. (*Math*)

Teacher Support

1. Assist with the graphing of bag options. If possible, discuss the value of each type of bag.

2. Provide opportunities for students to find pictures of foods and other groceries in magazines to decorate the store areas. Encourage students to draw signs and labels or to take pictures of items.

3. Determine how to obtain money to pay for services. Will students create money or credit cards, or earn play money in the classroom?

The Grocery Store *(cont.)*

Shopping List 2

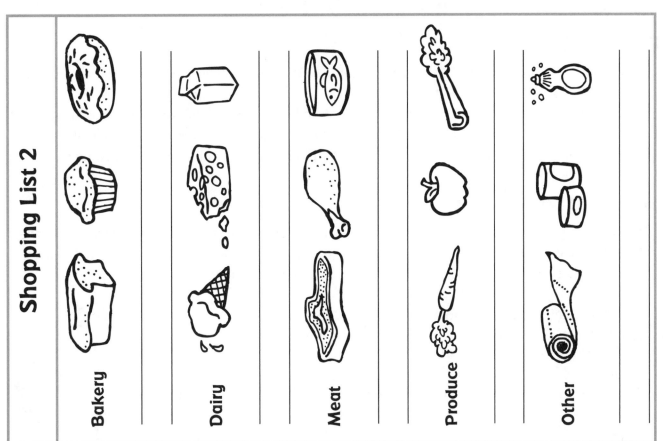

Bakery

Dairy

Meat

Produce

Other

Shopping List 1

The Grocery Store *(cont.)*

Phase 3: Define Roles

1. Construction is underway and the grocery store needs a staff and customers. Brainstorm different jobs and create a list of possible workers.

2. Discuss each job and list the responsibilities attached to it. What skills would each worker need? Will the workers dealing with customers have certain things to say? If so, plan a dialogue.

3. Figure out wardrobe items or props for each job. Find them in the classroom, borrow them, or make them.

Student STEM Activities

1. Research grocery store jobs, share data, and collect and display pictures. *(Technology/Engineering)*

2. Gather materials to create and store the wardrobe items and props for each role. Improvise and create additional props using classroom materials and imagination! *(Science/Technology/Engineering/Math)*

3. Create labels or name tags for each position. Consider making time sheets for workers and sign-up sheets for shoppers. *(Technology/Math)*

4. Dramatize different roles. Note how often math is used in a grocery store. Practice using scales to weigh produce, meat, and fish. Count and arrange items on shelves. Can the cans be stacked in pyramids? How tall can boxes be stacked before they fall over? How much can you fit in a bag? Add price tags and count money. Use a cash register or moneybox. *(Science/Technology/Engineering/Math)*

5. Practice writing shopping lists. Use word and picture cards to help. *(Engineering)*

Teacher Support

1. Review the list of jobs and their responsibilities, and provide wardrobe or prop ideas. Aprons or smocks would be appropriate in this center. Make other suggestions based on materials available.

2. Model the role of the shopper. Demonstrate how to create a grocery list, how to obtain money, how to locate items on the list, and how to use scales. You might wish to provide prepared word or picture shopping lists and ask the students to "shop" for specified items (a little like a scavenger hunt). Another idea might be to have students find five things that are red, or are vegetables, things in a can, boxed items, things that start with the letter "b," etc. and write what they are. **Note:** Many children will use developmental spelling, pretend writing, or draw what they want to buy. Encourage all appropriate efforts and provide as many writing cues as possible using word and picture cards. Also, point out that the names on boxes, cans, etc. can be copied, too.

3. Model the important role of stockers. Emphasize the necessity of returning items to the correct place in the store. Discuss how this helps the shopper locate the items on his or her list more easily.

4. Demonstrate the roles of the checkers and baggers. Explain UPC codes. Stress that good service is important. Also emphasize the benefits in taking turns.

The Grocery Store *(cont.)*

Phase 4: Open the Grocery Store

1. Discuss the best way to run the grocery store so things work smoothly. Make a list of all available jobs in the store.

2. If more than one strong suggestion has been made, form small groups to take turns doing trial runs of the different suggestions.

3. Vote for the best methods to implement and open for business.

Student STEM Activities

1. Practice and fine-tune systems for shopping, checking out, bagging, and stocking. Be aware that, once the store opens, changes and adjustments might be needed. *(Science/Technology/Engineering/Math)*

2. Figure out staffing and assign roles for the opening. Try to take turns with the different jobs.

   —How many checkers will work a shift? baggers? stock persons? deli- and bakery-counter workers?

   —How many customers can shop at a time? *(Engineering/Math)*

3. Work out time frames and create sign-up sheets. How long will shifts (turns) be? How long will the grocery store be opened (class period, all day)? *(Science/Technology/Engineering/Math)*

Teacher Support

1. Provide opportunities for research and discussion. Allow time and support for experimentation. Allow an extended period of time for the grand opening of the grocery store.

2. Explain the concept of *trial and error* and provide time for students to explore different options.

3. Listen to students brainstorm. Be aware of possible problems.

4. Once the newness of the shopping experience has worn off, focus students' attention on individual items in the store. Is the tomato fresh or frozen? In what food group does it belong? Does it need to be refrigerated? How did it get to the grocery store? Is it grown and trucked in from a farm?

The Grocery Store *(cont.)*

Phase 5: Improve the Grocery Store

1. Discuss what is working well in the grocery store. Is it easy to check out?

2. Analyze what needs fine-tuning.

3. Consider additions—adding UPC codes to products in the store, a delivery service, adding more items, staffing a deli, etc.

Student STEM Activities

1. Problem-solve to find better solutions to any difficulties mentioned in the brainstorming sessions.

   —Does the layout of the store and other counter areas work? Are more aisles needed?

   —Do the customers get good service? If not, what would improve the situation?

   —Are things easy to find and take off the shelves?

   —Are the displays appealing? Could they be improved with pictures, illustrations, or signs? *(Science/Technology/Engineering/Math)*

2. Collaborate and implement suggestions for improvement. Consider videotaping the store in action to review. *(Science/Technology/Engineering/Math)*

3. Enjoy the center. Continue collaborating and improving it. *(Science/Technology/Engineering/Math)*

4. Invite other classes to come in and enjoy shopping! *(Science/Technology/Engineering/Math)*

Teacher Support

1. Create a graphic organizer to list the responses to the student discussion.

2. Assist with problem solving.

3. Build upon student discoveries and encourage further study.

4. Take pictures of children in action. Print and bind them into a book. Use them for reference if reminders are needed for product placement. Later, use them to share what is happening in the classroom.

> **Note to Teachers:** The grocery store project can continue for days or weeks, be shared with other classes, or morph into something completely different.

STEM in Ice Fishing

cience

Biology—Learn more about fish. Are all fish the same? Are all fish edible? What is bait?

Nutrition and Health—Why do people catch fish? Are all fish healthy to eat?

Geography and Climate—Where do you go ice fishing? How is ice created? How is ice fishing different than fishing off of a dock or boat in warmer weather?

Safety—How can we protect ourselves from very cold temperatures while ice fishing? What is an ice shanty? How should fishing equipment and bait be handled?

echnology

Internet Research—Look for pictures of ice shanties. Search for different types of equipment used in ice fishing. Find geographic areas on a map where ice fishing is possible.

Desktop Publishing—Make copies of licenses and *Catch of the Day* recording sheets (page 78). Print pictures for display or reference. Create labels and name tags. Design advertising flyers.

ngineering

Drawing—Plan and map out the layout for the ice fishing area. Include areas for the fishing hole, an area for making/getting a license, a station for weighing and measuring the fish, and a space for students to record their catches.

Creating Spaces—Arrange the ice fishing area, licensing desk, and weigh stations.

Designing—Make an ice fishing area, fish, snow, and snowflakes. Can a more efficient fishing pole be made?

Collaborating and Problem Solving—Establish guidelines about how long a turn fishing will be and how many fish can be caught. Establish rules for taking turns, managing different areas, and what to do when finished fishing. Establish systems for weighing, measuring, and recording information about the day's catch.

ath

Numbers—Count the number of students who have been fishing, the number of fish caught each session, the number of fishing licenses sold, and the number of people who fish each session.

Sequencing—Arrange the fish in order by size, smallest to largest, or lightest to heaviest.

Size and Measurement—Weigh, measure, and chart the fish caught.

Addition and Subtraction—Add and subtract groups of fish, snowflakes, or fishing poles.

Market Research—Chart and graph the sizes of fish caught. Which size was caught the most? The least? Is there a most popular fish? Do more students prefer fishing on ice or during warmer weather?

Ice Fishing Starters

Suggested Props and Materials

- ◯ 5-gallon buckets
- ◯ cash register, calculator, and play money
- ◯ Catch of the Day recording sheet (page 78)
- ◯ clipboards
- ◯ fish patterns (page 80)
- ◯ Fishing License templates (page 83)
- ◯ foam core or white fabric cut to fit the top of the plastic pool
- ◯ glitter (white or silver)
- ◯ gloves
- ◯ hats
- ◯ large boxes
- ◯ magnets
- ◯ measurement cubes
- ◯ metal washers
- ◯ newsprint (white)
- ◯ paper clips
- ◯ pictures of fish
- ◯ plastic pool
- ◯ rulers
- ◯ scales
- ◯ shelving and tables
- ◯ small baskets
- ◯ stamp (fish) and stamp pads
- ◯ string or yarn
- ◯ timer
- ◯ wooden dowels

Others

_____

_____

_____

_____

_____

Ice Fishing Starters *(cont.)*

Vocabulary

agent	ice	tackle boxes
bait	length	weigh
balance scale	license	weight
cold	magnet	
compare	measure	
cooler	pole	
fish	reel	
fish and game	ruler	
fishing rod	shanty	
freeze	snow	

Others

_____

_____

_____

_____

_____

_____

_____

Books

Adventures with Jonny: Ice Fishing! The Coolest Sport on Earth by Michael Dilorenzo

Let's Go Fishing on the Ice by George Travis

Kitaq Goes Ice Fishing by Margaret Nicolai

Ice Fishing by Laura Purdie Salas

Others

_____

_____

_____

The Ice Fishing Plan

Phase 1: Set Up the Fishing Hole and the Ice Fishing Area

Students will:

- research and design an ice fishing area
- gather materials for the ice fishing area
- arrange a measuring and recording station
- establish a wall showing accomplishments such as heaviest fish, longest fish, or most fish in one session
- maintain a word wall
- name the ice fishing area and create signage

Phase 2: Create Ice Shanties, Fish, and Snow

Students will:

- graph experiences with fish and fishing
- use large boxes to create ice shanties
- cut out fish, and add paper clips and weights
- construct signs
- cut out paper snowflakes to hang in the area
- create snowdrifts

Phase 3: Define Roles

Students will:

- research types of workers needed to run an ice fishing area
- formulate job descriptions
- make personal fishing licenses
- determine the number of workers and fishermen; make sign-ups
- gather or make wardrobe items and prop materials
- practice fishing, weighing, and measuring the day's catch

Phase 4: Open the Ice Fishing Area

Students will:

- apply for a fishing license
- decide how many people can fish at a time and how long the fishing license will be valid each day (2–3 minutes a turn?)
- practice fishing (Try not to get poles tangled!)
- adjust procedures as needed and open the ice fishing business

Phase 5: Improve the Ice Fishing Area

Students will:

- discuss what is working and what needs adjusting
- initiate improvements based on discussions and research
- enjoy the newly created space and expand and improve as desired

Ice Fishing

Phase 1: Set Up the Fishing Hole and the Ice Fishing Area

1. Let's go ice fishing! What do we know about fishing in ice? What kinds of things do we need in order to create an ice fishing area and a weighing and measuring area?

2. Create lists of ideas and suggestions. What do we have that could be used? What do we need to find or borrow? Add to these organizational charts as the plan evolves.

3. Start a list of terms pertinent to ice fishing. Add to the list as the area takes shape.

4. Vote on a name for the ice fishing area.

Student STEM Activities

1. Research geographic areas that provide opportunities for ice fishing. Why is there ice in those locations? Collect pictures of fish and shanties. Share data. *(Science/Technology)*

2. Gather materials and classroom furniture (pool, white foam core or fabric, buckets or chairs, and fishing poles). Determine what is needed, what will fit, and where it will go. Create signage for the different areas.
(Science/Technology/Engineering/Math)

3. Construct the fishing hole with adult assistance. (See the illustration on page 74.) Add chairs or 5-gallon buckets (turned upside down) to sit on while fishing.
(Science/Technology/Engineering/Math)

4. Establish a station to weigh and measure the fish. Create a place to measure the length of the fish and another to determine the weight of the fish. Copy *Catch of the Day* sheets. (See page 78.) Create a counter where fishing licenses can be made. *(Science/Technology/Engineering/Math)*

5. Examine and measure real fish caught fishing, or the bait (minnows) used to catch fish. *(Science/Math)*

Teacher Support

1. Listen and record student responses during brainstorming sessions. Bring in live bait or fish that have been caught for students to examine.

2. Assist in cutting the holes for the fishing hole by covering a small wading pool with white fabric, paper, or foam core. The fishing holes should be eight inches in diameter.

3. Fill the classroom with related books and magazine or calendar pictures of fish. Be sure to include student contributions as they are created.

4. Review how the measurement tools can be used to measure the fish. Demonstrate how to fill out the *Catch of the Day* measurement data sheets.

5. Create word cards for a pocket chart or a word wall. Continue to add relevant vocabulary words as they come up. (See page 75.)

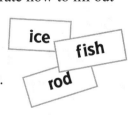

6. Ask parents to donate or gather materials and help with assembly of the center. Invite avid ice fishermen or women to come in and share their experiences.

Catch of the Day Recording Sheets

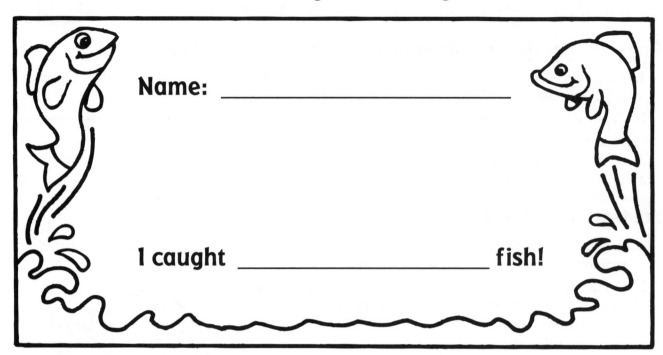

Name: _____

I caught _____ fish!

Directions: Use the ruler to measure the fish. Find the longest and shortest catch.

Name: _____

I caught _____ fish!

My *longest* fish was _____ long.

My *shortest* fish was _____ long.

1	2	3	4	5	6	7

Ice Fishing *(cont.)*

Phase 2: Create Ice Shanties, Fish, and Snow

1. Research ice-fishing shanties. Find out what they are used for and what they look like. Share data. Collect and display pictures. (See page 4.)

2. Share experiences. Who has gone fishing? Did you fish from a dock? on a boat? on ice?

Student STEM Activities

1. Graph responses to the fishing query and discuss the different experiences. What are some of the differences between fishing in water and fishing in water covered by ice? (***Technology/Math***)

2. Create one or more ice shanties using large appliance boxes. (***Engineering/Math***)

3. Make different-sized fish for the fishing hole. See page 80 for three-inch to seven-inch patterns. Laminate the fish. **Note:** Consider using a different color paper for each size fish to make it easier for sorting and graphing. (***Science/Technology/Math***)

4. Glue or tape weights (metal washers) to the backs of the fish and paperclips to the heads. Additional fish ideas can be found on the websites listed on page 8.
(***Science/Technology/Engineering/Math***)

5. Cut snowflakes to hang in the ice fishing area. Use the directions provided (page 81) or cut them free hand. Use glitter for added sparkle. (***Science/Technology/Engineering/Math***)

6. Crumple white newsprint, and secure it with tape to create the look of snow drifts around the fishing hole. You can also use white fabric over crumpled newspaper to create the drift effect.
(***Science/Technology/Engineering/Math***)

Teacher Support

1. Provide opportunities for students to talk about fishing experiences and to find fish and fishing pictures in magazines for decorating the area, or for signs and labels. Encourage students to design fish of their own and add weights.

2. Take pictures of students in the ice fishing area. Print and bind them into a class book. It can become a great way to share what is happening in the classroom with parents, and students love to see themselves in pictures!

Fish Patterns

How to Make a Snowflake

1. Start with a square sheet of white paper. Measure all four sides. They should be the same length.

2. Fold your square in half diagonally.

3. Fold your triangle in half diagonally.

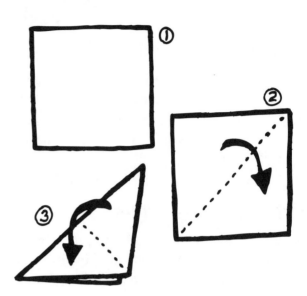

4. Fold paper in thirds—fold one side to the front and fold the other side to the back.

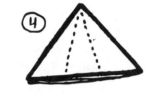

5. Snip the three corners off the folded paper.

6. Cut some fun designs along the sides of the folded paper.

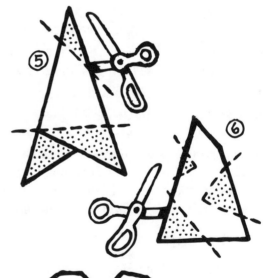

7. Unfold your paper, and look at your snowflake!

Ice Fishing *(cont.)*

Phase 3: Define Roles

1. Construction is underway and the ice fishing area needs a staff and customers. Brainstorm different jobs and create a list of possible workers.

2. Discuss each job and list the responsibilities attached to it. What skills might an ice fisherman need to be successful? What should the game agent do? Who will manage the weighing and measuring area?

3. Figure out wardrobe items or props for each job. Hats and gloves will work for those fishing.

Student STEM Activities

1. Research jobs related to ice fishing. Develop job descriptions. Collect and display pictures and share other data. *(Science/Engineering/Math)*

2. Gather materials to create and store the props and wardrobe items for each position. Improvise and create additional props needed using classroom materials and imagination! *(Science/Technology/Engineering/Math)*

3. Design labels or name tags for each position. Find or make fishing poles. Each should have a magnet on the end. *(Science/Technology/Engineering/Math)*

4. Make time sheets for workers. Create or print fishing awards. *(Technology/Engineering)*

5. Dramatize different roles within the center, and note how often math is used. Practice weighing and measuring fish. What about science? What do fishermen need to be aware of to go ice fishing safely? (weather conditions, thickness of ice) *(Science/Technology/Math)*

6. Make personal fishing licenses. Discuss why a license to fish is important. Sample licenses (page 83) and *Catch of the Day* measurement templates (page 78) are provided. Add school pictures or student-drawn self portraits to the box at the top right corner of the fishing licenses. *(Science/Technology/Engineering/Math)*

Teacher Support

1. Model the role of the Fish and Game Wardens and License Agents. One could be in charge of the people fishing, and the other in the office helping with the licenses. The person who will be a timer for those fishing might also be called an agent or warden. Review safety procedures for using the fishing poles. Provide wardrobe or prop ideas.

2. Assist with the assembly of the fishing rods. Have students hang the fishing poles upside down and attach the magnet (hook) to something metal like a filing cabinet. This will prevent tangling.

3. Review procedures for filling out license forms and also the *Catch of the Day* measurement sheets.

4. Take individual pictures of students and their catches. Enlarge the pictures and display them. Students can then compare their own "catch" to others! Provide opportunities for students to videotape themselves fishing or purchasing licenses.

Fishing Licenses

Fishing License

Name: _____

Address: _____

Monday	Tuesday	Wednesday	Thursday	Friday

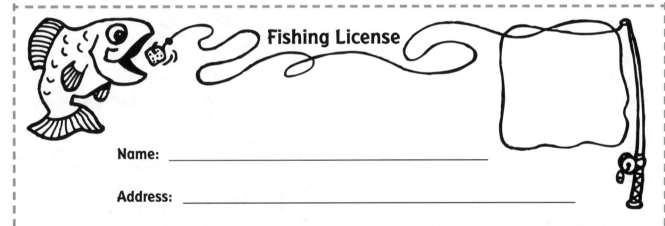

Fishing License

Name: _____

Address: _____

Monday	Tuesday	Wednesday	Thursday	Friday

Ice Fishing *(cont.)*

Phase 4: Open the Ice Fishing Area

1. Discuss the best way to run the ice fishing area. Should a timer be used to help switch roles?

2. How will students choose jobs and sign up for fishing opportunities?

3. If more than one strong suggestion has been made, form small groups to take turns doing trial runs of the different suggestions.

4. Vote for the best methods to implement ideas and open for business.

Student STEM Activities

1. Practice and fine-tune a system for stamping licenses, fishing, and weighing and measuring the catches each day. *(Science/Technology/Engineering/Math)*

2. Figure out staffing and assign roles for the opening.

    —How many workers will be needed to work a shift? Fish and Game agents?

    —How many students can fish at a time?

    —Should the fishing licenses be bought? How might they be paid for?
    (Technology/Math)

3. Work out time frames. Create sign-up sheets. How long will the center be opened (class period, all day)? How long will shifts (turns) be? How will they be timed? *(Technology/Math)*

Teacher Support

1. Provide opportunities for research and discussion. Allow time and support for experimentation. Allow an extended period of time for the grand opening of the ice fishing area.

2. Explain the concept of *trial and error* and provide time for students to explore different options.

3. Let the center get established. Once all students have had chances to fish, redirect their focus to finding out more about ice fishing (science) and encourage them to spend more time weighing, measuring, and comparing their catches.

Ice Fishing *(cont.)*

Phase 5: Improve the Ice Fishing Area

1. Discuss what is working well.

2. Analyze what needs fine-tuning or improving.

3. Consider adding more fish in different lengths or weights or increasing the number of shanties.

Student STEM Activities

1. Problem-solve to find better solutions to difficulties mentioned during brainstorming.

   —Does the layout of the area work? If not, how could it be rearranged?

   —Do the fishing rods work? If not, what would improve them? *(Engineering/Math)*

2. Collaborate and implement suggestions for improvement. *(Science/Technology/Engineering/Math)*

3. Enjoy the center. Continue collaborating and improving it. *(Science/Technology/Engineering/Math)*

Teacher Support

1. Create a graphic organizer to list the responses to the student discussion.

2. Assist with problem solving for issues that arise.

3. Analyze the data from the graph of the sizes of fish caught. Pose questions about why the amounts were the way they were.

Supplemental Activities

1. Find an adult who can catch, prepare, and serve fish he or she caught. Make a graph of whether students liked the fish or not, or had ever eaten it or not.

2. Add alphabet letters to the fish. The students could try to catch each letter of the alphabet and record it, catch six letters and see if they can make a word, sort capital and lowercase letters, sort consonants and vowels, etc. The literacy opportunities are limitless.

3. Consider growing Snow Crystals while the Ice Fishing center is in use. See page 86 for directions and materials needed.

Note: The ice fishing project can continue for days or weeks, become a permanent fixture, or morph into something else entirely. Student interest will determine its continuing value.

Growing Snow Crystals

Supplies

- ammonia
- bluing
- charcoal briquettes
- distilled water
- food coloring
- uniodized salt

Utensils

- empty jar
- glass or plastic pie plate
- measuring spoons
- eye dropper

Directions

1. Place charcoal in an even layer in the pie plate.

2. Sprinkle distilled water onto charcoal until it is thoroughly damp. Pour off any excess water.

3. In an empty jar, mix 3 Tbs. uniodized salt, 3 Tbs. ammonia, and 6 Tbs. bluing. Stir until the salt is dissolved.

4. Pour the mixture over the prepared dampened charcoal.

5. Swirl a bit of water around in the emptied jar to pick up the remaining chemicals and pour this liquid onto the charcoal.

6. Add drops of food coloring across the surface of the "charcoal garden." Areas with no food coloring will be white.

7. Sprinkle more salt (about 2 Tbs.) across the surface of the garden.

8. Set the garden in an area where it will not be disturbed.

9. On days 2 and 3, pour an additional mixture of ammonia, water, and bluing (2 Tbs. each) in the bottom of the pan, being careful not to disturb the delicate growing crystals.

10. Keep the pan in an undisturbed place, but check on it periodically to watch your garden grow!

STEM in the Pizza Parlor

cience

Nutrition and Health—Find out where different pizza ingredients come from. How are they prepared? Are some more nutritious than others?

Chemistry/Cooking—In cooking, ingredients are mixed together to form something new. Does the order in which ingredients are mixed matter? What happens when food is heated?

Hygiene and Safety—Find out why restaurant workers need to wash their hands and/or cover their hair and why refrigeration is important.

echnology

Internet Research—Find recipes, ingredient information, and menu ideas for pizzas; search for ideas to arrange and decorate the pizza parlor; learn about relevant pizza-making tools and machinery; find ideas for ovens and other possible props.

Desktop Publishing—Create labels, name tags, order sheets, menus and invitations; design advertising flyers or a field trip announcement.

ngineering

Drawing—Plan and map out the layout for the pizza parlor. Include areas for dining, prep, and cooking.

Creating Spaces—Arrange the pizza parlor using tables, chairs, shelving, and other materials at hand.

Designing—Make a pizza oven, a large spatula (peel), and/or a refrigerator.

Collaborating and Problem Solving—Determine how the prep area should be set up, who will work it, and who will serve the food. Establish a pizza-making "assembly line" and adjust as needed.

ath

Numbers—Count the toppings on a slice, the number of pizzas, the number of patrons, workers, chairs, etc.

Sequencing—In what order are pizza ingredients combined? (*crust* ➜ *sauce* ➜ *toppings*); what other sequences are part of working in a restaurant? (*ordering food* ➜ *preparing food* ➜ *serving food*)

Size and Measurement—Focus on odd or even; greater than or less than; small, medium, large, extra large; heavy, light.

Addition and Subtraction—Compute the number of pizzas sold or pizza toppings added.

Money—Establish prices, compute the amount of a bill, and make change.

Market Research—Chart and graph favorite toppings, the number of pizzas served each session, the number of customers per visit, etc.

Pizza Parlor Starters

⊢■—■—■—■— Suggested Props and Materials —■—■—■—■⊣

- ◯ aprons and oven mitts

- ◯ cardboard boxes (to make pizza oven, refrigerator, prep areas, hostess station, etc.)

- ◯ cardboard circles for pizza bases (crust)

- ◯ cash register or box; play money; calculator

- ◯ kitchen furnishings (student-sized stove, sink, cupboards, oven, tables, chairs)

- ◯ patterns for pizza toppings (pages 93–94)

- ◯ pizza boxes

- ◯ pizza order sheets (pages 95–96)

- ◯ red and white paint for pizzas

- ◯ shoe boxes or plastic bins for storing toppings

- ◯ utensils

- ◯ Velcro circles for pizza toppings

Others

_____

_____

_____

_____

Pizza Parlor Starters *(cont.)*

Vocabulary

busboy	hostess	prep cook
chef	manager	reservation
cheese	maitre d'	restaurant
consumer	menu	toppings
cook	oven	sauce
crust	parlor	server
customer	patron	supplier
dough	pizza	waiter
dishwasher	peel	waitress
grower		

Others

_____
_____
_____
_____
_____
_____

Books

Pete's a Pizza by William Steig

Curious George and the Pizza Party by H.A. Rey

The Little Red Hen Makes a Pizza by Philemon Sturges

Hi, Pizza Man! by Virginia Walter

The Princess and the Pizza by Mary Jane and Herm Auch

Others

_____
_____
_____
_____

The Pizza Parlor Plan

Phase 1: Set Up the Pizza Parlor

Students will:

- research and design a classroom pizza parlor
- gather and arrange pizza parlor materials
- create a pizza oven and other related items
- maintain a word wall
- vote on a name for the pizza parlor and create signage

Phase 2: Make Pizza, Toppings, and Menus

Students will:

- research pizza and toppings and their origins
- graph or chart favorite toppings
- create "prop" pizzas using cardboard, paint, Velcro, and patterns
- construct menus and order sheets
- make and maintain an inventory list for pizzas, toppings, etc.

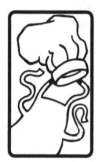

Phase 3: Define Roles

Students will:

- research types of workers needed to run a pizza parlor
- formulate job descriptions
- gather or make wardrobe items and prop materials
- determine the number of workers and customers; make sign-ups
- practice taking and placing orders and using money

Phase 4: Open the Pizza Parlor

Students will:

- discuss ways to assemble pizza orders and vote on the best method
- organize a pizza-preparation area in the pizza parlor
- practice pizza assembly using the pizzas and toppings
- open the pizza parlor for business and implement the plans

Phase 5: Improve the Pizza Parlor

Students will:

- evaluate what worked and what needs adjusting
- initiate improvements based on discussions and research
- enjoy the newly created space and expand and improve as desired

The Pizza Parlor

Phase 1: Set Up the Pizza Parlor

1. Let's make a pizza parlor! What do we know about pizza parlors? What do we need to set one up? What do we have that could be used? What do we need to find and/or borrow?

2. Create webs or lists of ideas and suggestions. (Have students add to these organizational charts as they become more involved in the planning.)

3. Review the list of terms pertinent to the pizza parlor. Add to it as interest grows.

4. Vote on a name for the class pizza parlor.

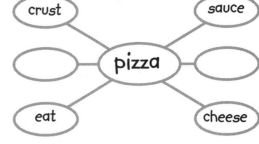

Student STEM Activities

1. Research pizza parlors and provide pictures when possible. Share data and map out a plan. *(Technology/Engineering/Math)*

2. Gather materials and classroom furniture to set up the pizza parlor based on the maps and brainstorming sessions. Determine what is needed, what will fit, and where it will go. *(Technology/Engineering/Math)*

3. Collaborate and create a pizza oven and a sign for the pizza parlor. Improvise, arrange, and embellish items to create the pizza parlor space. *(Technology/Engineering/Math)*

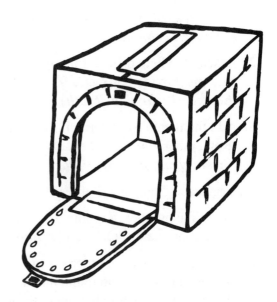

Teacher Support

1. Listen to and record student responses during brainstorming sessions. Offer encouragement and guidance when appropriate.

2. Fill the classroom with related books, word cards, sample menus, pictures, and posters. Include student contributions as they are created.

3. Create word cards for a pocket chart or a word wall. See page 89 for suggestions. Continue to add relevant vocabulary words as suggested.

4. Call local restaurants for donations (napkins, hats, aprons, menus, etc.). Find out if these restaurants will accommodate a field trip. Some will let children come in and make their own pizzas or donate dough for class pizza-making parties.

5. Ask parents to donate or gather materials or help with cutting or assembly to get the Pizza Parlor going. Invite parents in related industries to come in and share their work experiences.

The Pizza Parlor *(cont.)*

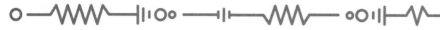

Phase 2: Make Pizza, Toppings, and Menus

1. Graph favorite pizza toppings and determine the top four. Discuss the origin of each topping.

2. Plan the pizza menu based on the top four pizza toppings. Consider some combination pizzas.

Favorite Pizza Toppings			
		X	X
	X	X	X
X	X	X	X
pepperoni	**olive**	**mushroom**	**sausage**

Student STEM Activities

1. Find out how pizza sauce is made. Paint cardboard circles red (sauce), but try to leave the outer rim unpainted (crust). When the red paint is dry, add white dots or squiggles (cheese). When the white paint is dry, add small Velcro circles to the tops of the "pizzas." *(Science/Technology)*

2. Research where different ingredients originate. Prepare pizza toppings using the patterns provided on pages 93–94. Hand-draw other toppings as needed. *(Science/Technology/Math)*

3. Add the matching Velcro circles to the backs of each of the toppings. (Remember, one half of each Velcro pair is on the painted pizza circles.) *(Science/Engineering/Math)*

4. Organize a "prep area" and a storage system for the toppings. *(Engineering)*

5. Count the number of toppings in each container and list the number on the front label. *(Technology/Math)*

6. Construct menus and order sheets. Take pictures of each pizza ordered, and add them to the menu or draw the different pizzas. Determine prices for the menu. Print copies. *(Technology/Math)*

Teacher Support

1. Prepare a pizza topping graph. Focus students' attention on where each item comes from, and what is entailed in getting it to the restaurant. Does it need to be grown and trucked in from a farm, processed, or purchased in bulk from a store? Could it come straight from a garden, like a tomato, or does something have to be done to it first, like pepperoni? And just what is pepperoni?

2. Enlist parents to help cut and prepare *some* of the toppings. Use felt scraps or laminated pieces of construction paper to create more lasting toppings.

3. Provide opportunities for students to cut out some of the toppings. If they wish to draw some of their own or add pictures, provide circle patterns for them to use as a base. Laminate the additional toppings to be cut out.

4. Obtain shoebox-sized boxes to create prep-area bins for storing toppings and cardboard circles for the pizza base.

5. Establish areas to paint and dry the pizza circles and to cut out the toppings.

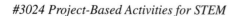

The Pizza Parlor *(cont.)*

Color and copy the toppings and laminate them. Review where each topping comes from and how it is prepared. Have students (and parent helpers) cut out the pizza topping circles. Add Velcro circles to the backs of the toppings. The other Velcro half will be added to the painted cardboard pizza circles.

pepperoni	green peppers	olives	cheese

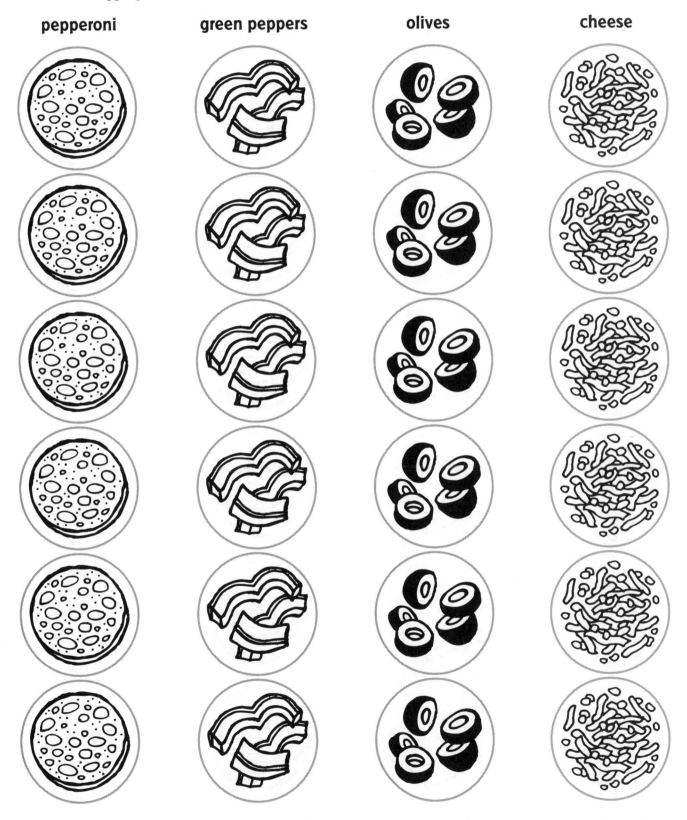

The Pizza Parlor *(cont.)*

Color and copy the toppings and laminate them. Review where each topping comes from and how it is prepared. Have students (and parent helpers) cut out the pizza topping circles. Add Velcro circles to the back of the toppings. The other Velcro half will be added to the painted cardboard pizza circles.

ham	pineapple	onions	sausage

_____ **Pizza Parlor**

Circle each topping that you want to order.

Cheese

Mushrooms

Olives

Onions

Pepperoni

Sausage

Number of Toppings   1   2   3   4   5   6

_____ **Pizza Parlor**

Check each topping that you want to order.

Cheese  ☐

Mushrooms  ☐

Olives  ☐

Onions  ☐

Pepperoni  ☐

Sausage  ☐

Circle the number of toppings.

| 1 | 2 | 3 | 4 | 5 | 6 |

Circle the price of the pizza.

1 Topping	2 Toppings	3 Toppings	4 Toppings	5 Toppings	6 Toppings
$1.00	$2.00	$3.00	$4.00	$5.00	$6.00

The Pizza Parlor *(cont.)*

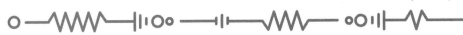

Phase 3: Define Roles

1. Construction is underway and the pizza parlor needs a staff and customers! Let's brainstorm different pizza parlor jobs and create a list of possible workers.

2. Discuss each job and list the responsibilities attached to it. What skills would each worker need to be successful? Will the workers dealing with customers have certain things to say? If so, plan dialogue.

3. Figure out wardrobe items or props for each job.

4. Discuss hygiene in a restaurant. Include hand washing and keeping the cooking implements in a restaurant clean.

Student STEM Activities

1. Research pizza parlor jobs and share data. Collect and display pictures. *(Technology/Engineering)*

2. Gather materials to create and store the props and wardrobe items for each position. Improvise to create additional props needed using classroom materials and imagination! *(Science/Technology/Engineering/Math)*

3. Create labels or name tags for each position. Consider making time sheets for workers and reservations, and sign-in sheets for patrons. *(Technology/Math)*

4. Act out different pizza parlor roles. Note how often math and science are used in a pizza parlor. *(Science/Technology/Engineering/Math)*

5. Practice using money and a cash register or a moneybox. *(Technology/Math)*

6. Review hand-washing procedures. Research other restaurant hygiene and safety practices and incorporate them. Adjust restaurant layout as needed. *(Science/Technology/Engineering)*

Teacher Support

1. Review the list of jobs and their responsibilities, and provide wardrobe or prop ideas. Perhaps suggest that chefs' hats, or *toques*, be made and worn by the cooks, or make other suggestions based on materials available.

2. Model the role of the waiter/waitress. Demonstrate how to take an order and bring it to the cook. Use one of the sample order sheets provided until students are comfortable creating their own.

3. Discuss the importance of listening to the customers and writing orders clearly. Good service and manners are important!

4. Review proper hygiene and safety practices.

The Pizza Parlor *(cont.)*

Phase 4: Open the Pizza Parlor

1. Discuss the best way to assemble each pizza. Should there be more than one prep cook? Will an assembly line work? Should pizzas be made one at a time, or should different people have different tasks for each pizza?

2. If more than one strong suggestion has been made, form small groups to take turns doing trial runs of the different suggestions.

3. Vote for the best assembly method to implement and open for business.

Student STEM Activities

1. Take turns making pizzas in the pizza parlor. *(Science/Engineering/Math)*

2. Practice and fine-tune a system that all can agree upon. Be aware that, once the pizza parlor opens, changes and adjustments might be needed. *(Engineering)*

3. Document the pizza-making process. Post pictures or posters of the process, or make a "training" video. *(Technology/Engineering)*

4. Figure out staffing and assign roles for the opening. Create sign-up sheets.

   —How many waiters will work a shift?

   —How many customers can be seated at a time? *(Technology/Engineering/Math)*

5. Open for business.

   —How long will the pizza parlor be open (class period, all day)?

   —How long will shifts (turns) be? *(Technology/Engineering/Math)*

Teacher Support

1. Provide opportunities for practice and discussion. Allow time and support for experimentation. Allow an extended period of time for the opening of the pizza parlor.

2. Encourage students to try different methods of pizza preparation. Review the concept of *trial and error* if necessary and provide time for students to explore different options.

3. Listen to student brainstorming sessions. Provide guidance when needed.

4. Review proper hygiene and safety practices.

The Pizza Parlor *(cont.)*

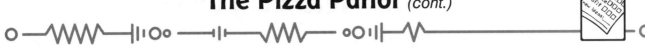

Phase 5: Improve the Pizza Parlor

1. Discuss what is working well.

2. Analyze what needs fine-tuning.

3. Consider additions—delivery service, cooking show, additional menu items, sizes, etc.

Student STEM Activities

1. Problem-solve to find better solutions to any difficulties mentioned in the brainstorming sessions.

   —Does the layout of the restaurant and the prep area work? If not, how could it be rearranged?

   —Does the pizza preparation plan (sequencing) work? If not, what needs to be adjusted and why?

   —Do the customers get good service? If not, what would improve the situation? *(Engineering)*

2. Collaborate to implement suggestions for improvement. *(Science/Technology/Engineering/Math)*

3. Enjoy the center. Continue collaborating and improving it.
   (Science/Technology/Engineering/Math)

Teacher Support

1. Create a graphic organizer to list the responses to the student discussion.

Worked	Needs More Work	Solutions

2. Assist with problem solving.

> **Note to Teachers:** This project can continue for days or weeks, become a permanent fixture, or morph into something else entirely. Student interest will determine its continuing value.

STEM in the Veterinary Clinic

science

Nutrition and Health—What do animals need to be healthy? Are their needs the same as humans? Do all animals eat the same things?

Hygiene and Safety—Why is it important to keep things clean in the office? How do veterinarians take care of larger animals that cannot be seen in the office? Do animals need shots?

technology

Internet Research—Search for ideas to arrange and decorate the veterinary clinic. Learn about relevant tools needed when examining pets, taking care of injuries, or performing surgeries. Find ideas for possible props.

Desktop Publishing—Make copies of registration sheets and patient charts. Find pictures of animals and equipment to use for display or reference. Create labels and name tags, and design advertising flyers.

engineering

Drawing—Plan the layout for the veterinary clinic. Include a waiting area, an examination room, and an area for surgery.

Creating Spaces—Arrange the office using classroom furniture and materials at hand. Create other items as needed.

Designing—Create a reception area and pet beds and carriers. Gather or make veterinarian's instruments.

Collaborating and Problem Solving—Determine how the areas within the office should be set up and what services will be provided. How many doctors, nurses, and assistants will work at a time? What kinds of animals will be serviced in the clinic and how many pet owners can be in the waiting room at a time?

math

Numbers—Count and classify the animals that are seen each day. Tally the number of paws or tails, and the number of procedures. Make Venn diagrams comparing different animals.

Sequencing—In what order are the patients seen? What is the sequence of steps during an examination? What happens after the visit is over?

Size and Measurement—Measure and record the length of the pets using rulers. Use scales to weigh animals. Record and compare findings.

Addition and Subtraction—Compute the number of services provided for each pet. How many pets are seen in a certain time period? How many similar or different ailments are diagnosed?

Money—Establish prices, compute the amount of a bill, and practice making change.

Market Research—Chart and graph the kinds of animals seen and the types of procedures provided.

Veterinary Clinic Starters

Suggested Props and Materials

- ◯ animal magazines and catalogs
- ◯ animal X-rays
- ◯ bandages
- ◯ boxes for pet crates
- ◯ clipboards
- ◯ doctor's tools (pretend)— stethoscopes, needles (shots), thermometers
- ◯ empty medicine containers
- ◯ fabric, fabric strips, ribbon, twine
- ◯ file folders for patient charts
- ◯ gauze
- ◯ medical smocks
- ◯ Pet Name Tags templates (page 106)
- ◯ old blankets and towels
- ◯ paper for tags and collars
- ◯ pet cages and carriers
- ◯ pictures of animals
- ◯ pictures of students and their pets (or with stuffed animals)
- ◯ Pet Chart template (page 106)
- ◯ Pet Checkup template (page 108)
- ◯ rulers, measuring tapes
- ◯ scales
- ◯ stuffed, plastic, or rubber animals
- ◯ tongue depressors

Others

_____

_____

_____

_____

* Many veterinary clinics are happy to donate or loan materials to classrooms.

Veterinary Clinic Starters *(cont.)*

Vocabulary

	female	thermometer
	fleas	vaccine
	fur	vet
	groom	veterinarian
animal	healthy	weigh
assistant	leash	wild
bath	length	X-rays
care	male	
carrier	ruler	
claws	scale	**Others**
clinic	scales	_____
collar	stethoscope	_____
domestic	stitches	_____
		_____

Books

What Happens at a Vet's Office? by Amy Hutchings

Veterinarians Help Keep Animals Healthy by Bobbie Kalman

I Want to Be a Veterinarian by Stephanie Maze

Veterinarians in Our Community by Michelle Ames

A Day with Animal Doctors by Leonie Bennett

A Day in the Life of a Veterinarian by Heather Adamson

Others

_____

_____

_____

_____

The Veterinary Clinic Plan

Phase 1: Set up the Veterinary Clinic

Students will:

- graph experiences at a veterinary clinic
- research which types of animals go to a veterinary clinic and which types of animals have veterinarians go to them
- gather and arrange materials to create a space for examining animals, a table for performing surgery, and a waiting room
- maintain a word wall
- vote on a name for the veterinary clinic and create signage

Phase 2: Create Crates, Beds, Collars, Leashes, and ID Tags

Students will:

- research equipment used by veterinarians and create similar items
- create crates and carriers for dogs, cats, etc. to stay in at the clinic
- measure pets to make pet collars and leashes

Phase 3: Define Roles

Students will:

- research veterinarians and other workers needed in a veterinary clinic
- formulate job descriptions; try different roles; make sign-ups
- gather or make wardrobe and prop materials
- create charts for pets
- practice caring for animal patients

Phase 4: Open the Veterinary Clinic

Students will:

- discuss ways to carry out certain procedures and vote on the best methods
- practice weighing and measuring pets
- do a trial run with clients, workers, and medical personnel, and adjust as needed
- open the clinic for business and implement the plans that have been formulated

Phase 5: Improve the Veterinary Clinic

Students will:

- evaluate what worked and what needs adjusting
- initiate improvements based on discussions and research
- enjoy the newly created space and expand and improve as desired

The Veterinary Clinic

Phase 1: Set up the Veterinary Clinic

1. Let's open a veterinary clinic! What do we know about them? Have you ever brought your pet to a veterinarian for care?

Have You Gone to a Vet?										
Yes										
No										

2. What kinds of things do we need in order to create a clinic for animals? What do we have, and what do we need to find and/or borrow? Create lists of ideas and organizational charts.

3. Start a list of terms pertinent to the veterinary clinic. Add to the list as the clinic takes shape. Post the words so students can copy them as needed.

4. Vote on a name for the veterinary clinic.

Student STEM Activities

1. Research, classify, and draw different types of animals. Determine which types of animals will be treated in the clinic—domestic, wild, or both. Print or draw pictures. Share data and create signage. (*Science/Technology/Math*)

2. Draw maps to plan area. Gather boxes, animals, doctor's tools, and classroom furniture and begin setting up the clinic based on brainstorming sessions. (*Science/Technology/Engineering/Math*)

3. Construct and arrange specific areas for examining animals, a surgery bed, office areas for scheduling and payment, and appropriate waiting areas for animals and pet owners. (*Science/Technology/Engineering/Math*)

4. Survey the animals collected for use in the clinic. Make a chart to show how many of each there are. Use this information to create appropriate crates and kennels. (*Science/Technology/Engineering/Math*)

Teacher Support

1. Fill the classroom with related books, word cards, and magazine pictures of animals (both domesticated and wild); collect pictures of students and their pets and posters. Include student contributions as they are created.

2. Create word cards for a pocket chart or a word wall. (See page 102.) Continue to add relevant vocabulary words when appropriate.

3. Focus students' attention on individual instruments such as stethoscopes, thermometers, and needles (shots). Discuss how and why they are used.

4. Call local veterinarians for donations or loans (X-rays, pictures, appointment cards, business cards, expired pet magazines). Find out if they will accommodate field trips.

5. Ask parents to donate or gather materials, or to help with assembly or construction to get the veterinary clinic started. Invite a veterinarian or assistant to come in and share their experiences.

The Veterinary Clinic (cont.)

Phase 2: Create Crates, Beds, Collars, Leashes, and ID Tags

1. Share information about family pets. Do you have a pet? How many pets do you have? What kind of pet? Is it a male or female?

2. Discuss how to take care of different animals. When should you take it to a veterinary clinic?

3. Talk about ways to get animals to a clinic and crates to keep them safe from other animals while at the veterinary clinic.

Student STEM Activities

1. Take a class poll of the pets classmates have. Classify them, and then graph or chart them. (*Science/Technology/Math*)

2. Use boxes and other materials to create crates, beds, and carriers for the pets that will visit the class veterinary clinic. Figure out ways to stack the crates for animals staying overnight. Fill them with materials to make the beds soft. (*Engineering/Math*)

3. Measure the necks of pets needing collars and leashes. Craft the collars and leashes using lengths of fabric, twine, or other materials. Later, compare the different lengths and determine which animals had the smallest, largest, etc. (*Science/Technology/Engineering/Math*)

4. Make name tags (or use the ones on page 106) to be used on collars and crates. Put the name of the pet, the type of animal, and other important information. (*Science/Technology/Engineering/Math*)

Teacher Support

1. Participate in student discussions about pets and pet care.

2. Provide guidance, if needed, with classifying types of pets or other animals. Assist with graphing and charts.

3. Assist with finding materials and with measuring to make different pet items.

4. Offer encouragement and provide reasonable amounts of time for research, planning, measuring, and creating.

The Veterinary Clinic *(cont.)*

Pet Name Tags

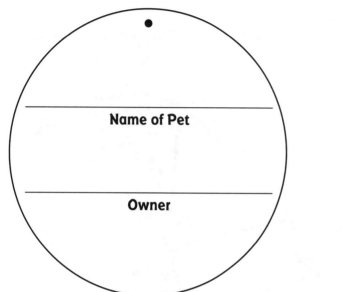

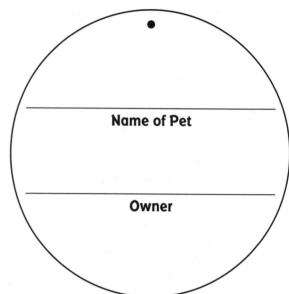

Name of Pet

Owner

Name of Pet

Owner

Pet Chart

Name of Pet: _____

Type of Animal: Circle or color the animal you are bringing in.

cat

dog

rabbit

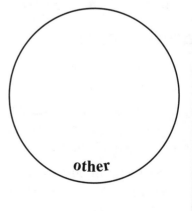

other

snake

bird

guinea pig

©Teacher Created Resources

The Veterinary Clinic *(cont.)*

Phase 3: Define Roles

1. Discuss a veterinarian's job and other workers at a veterinary clinic. Will you have pet walkers or pet groomers? What skills would each worker need to be successful? Is science important?

2. What tools might a vet use? What are X-rays for? What tools will other workers need?

3. Look at a real or stuffed dog. During a healthy dog or cat check up, a veterinarian will check the dog from nose-to-tail. What does this mean? Review body parts—*nose, ears, eyes, mouth, stomach, paws, tail.*

Student STEM Activities

1. Research veterinarians and animal care. Share data. Collect and display pictures. *(Science/Technology/Engineering/Math)*

2. Determine wardrobe items or props for each job. Create labels or name tags for each position in the veterinary clinic. Find them in the classroom, borrow them, or make them. *(Technology/Engineering)*

3. Make time sheets for workers. Figure out shifts. *(Technology/Engineering/Math)*

4. Dramatize different roles. Practice looking at X-rays, holding and caring for pets, and doing office work. Think about ways to calm worried pet owners. *(Science/Technology/Engineering/Math)*

5. Create pet name tags and charts (or use the ones on page 106) to have available for pet owners to fill out before they see the veterinarian. Print copies. *(Science/Technology/Engineering/Math)*

Teacher Support

1. Explain the concept of a healthy pet checkup and the meaning of a nose-to-tail check. Share the Pet Check Up template (page 108) if it is to be used.

2. Introduce the X-rays. If you are unable to obtain a light table, they can be held up to a window. Figure out what kind of an animal is shown on each one.

3. Model the role of the pet owner. Discuss care for different types of animals.

4. Model the roles of veterinarians and assistants. Emphasize the importance of care and kindness to the animals and their owners. Stress that good service is always important.

Pet Checkup

Pet Name: _____

Owner: _____

Type of Animal: _____

Length: _____

Nose-to-Tail Check

nose

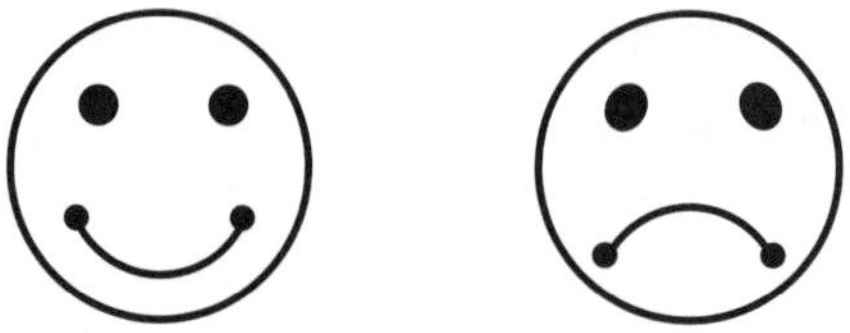

eyes

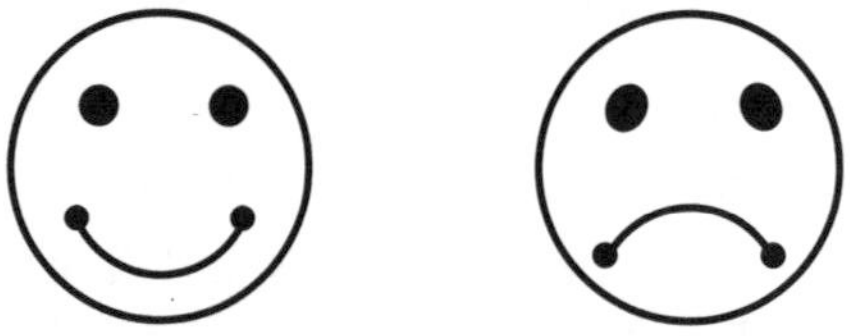

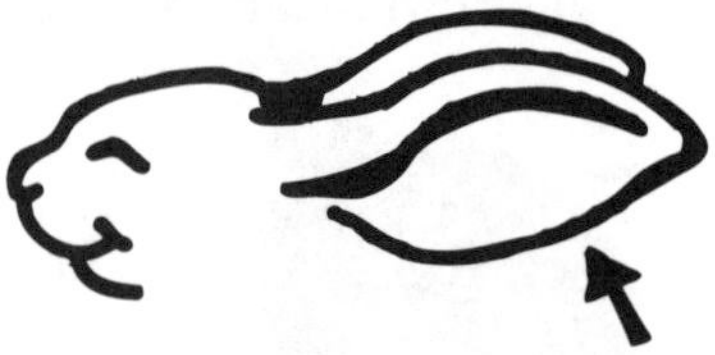

ears

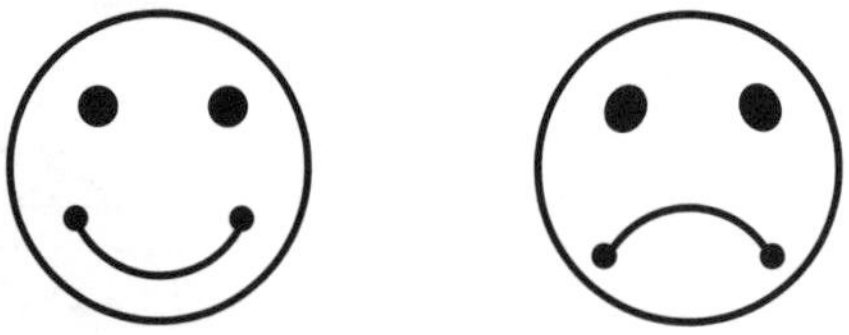

mouth

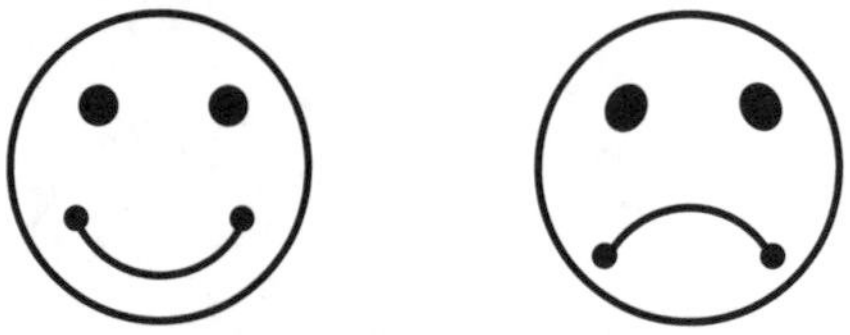

stomach

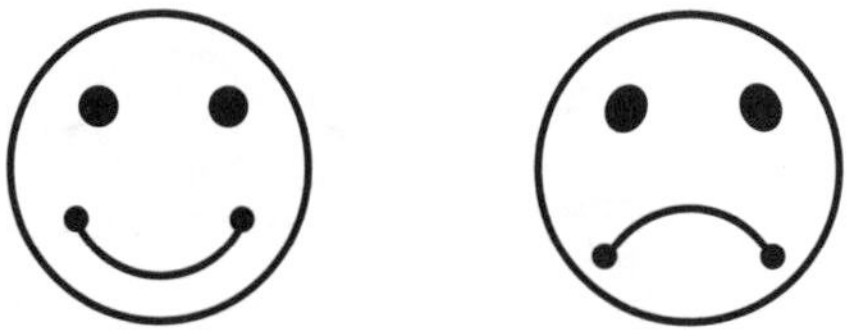

paws

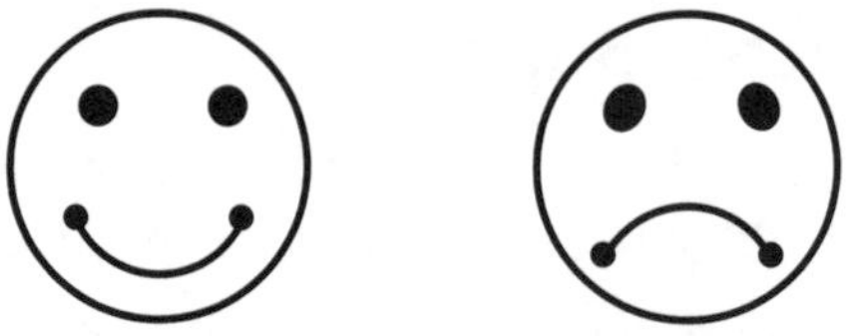

tail

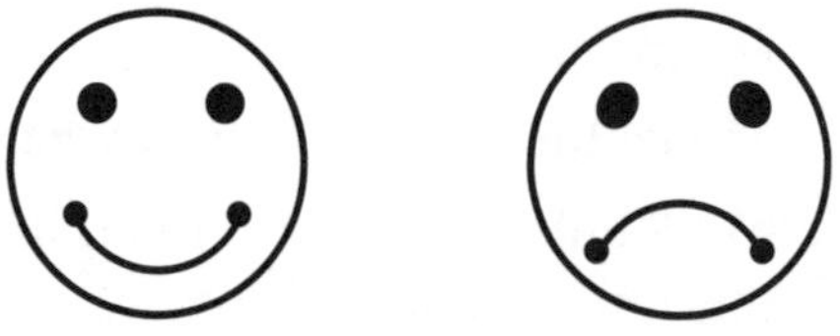

The Veterinary Clinic *(cont.)*

Phase 4: Open the Veterinary Clinic

1. Choose a stuffed animal to use as a pet. Introduce your pet. Make sure the animals are the type that would be seen in a veterinary clinic. Remember, veterinarians make house calls to check large animals like gorillas, zebras, cows, pigs, etc. Those animals are too big and wild for office visits!

2. Discuss fees for different services. Don't forget that pets staying at the clinic will need food and water. Will they need to be walked too?

3. Form small groups to take turns being veterinarians, technicians, office workers, and pet owners.

Student STEM Activities

1. Decide upon prices for different clinic services, and make a chart or sign. *(Technology/Math)*

2. Practice and fine-tune systems for measuring the length of each pet and for taking X-rays. Be aware that once the office opens, changes and adjustments might be needed. *(Science/Technology/Engineering/Math)*

3. Figure out staffing and assign roles for the opening.
   —How many workers will be needed to work a shift? Veterinarians? Assistants? Receptionists? X-ray technicians?
   —How many pet owners can be seen at a time? *(Engineering/Math)*

4. Work out time frames. Create sign-up sheets. How long will the veterinary clinic be open—a class period, all day? How long will shifts (turns) be? *(Technology/Math)*

Teacher Support

1. Provide opportunities for research and discussion of different animals and procedures. Allow time and support for experimentation. Allow an extended period of time for the grand opening of the veterinary clinic.

2. Explain the concept of *trial and error* and provide time for students to explore different options. Consider rotating the types of animals being cared for.

3. Review safety procedures used in a veterinary clinic and while working around animals.

4. Listen to student brainstorming sessions. Be aware of possible problems.

The Veterinary Clinic *(cont.)*

Phase 5: Improve the Veterinary Clinic

1. Discuss what is working well in the clinic. Do all the animals have comfortable resting places? Analyze what needs fine-tuning.

2. Consider additions—grooming, boarding, etc. Is it time to have veterinarians service large animals at their locations, such as a class zoo or farm?

Student STEM Activities

1. Problem-solve to find better solutions to any difficulties mentioned in the brainstorming sessions.

   —Does the layout of the clinic work? If not, how could it be rearranged?

   —Do the animals get good care? If not, what would improve the situation?
   (Science/Engineering/Math)

2. Collaborate and implement suggestions for improvement. ***(Science/Technology/Engineering/Math)***

3. Enjoy the center. Continue collaborating and improving it. ***(Science/Technology/Engineering/Math)***

Teacher Support

1. Take pictures of pet owners and their pets to post in the clinic or put in a class book to share.

2. Assist with problem solving for issues that arose.

3. Pose problems that might occur in a real clinic, such as, what happens if an animal gets loose?

4. Create a graphic organizer to list the responses to the student discussion for possible additions or extensions to the area.

Worked	Needs More Work	Solutions

Note to Teachers: The veterinary clinic project can continue for days or weeks, become a permanent fixture, or morph into something else entirely. Student interest will determine its continuing value.